£2.50

# ITALIAN
# IN THREE MONTHS

HUGO'S LANGUAGE BOOKS LTD
LONDON

ISBN 0 85285 053 0


*3rd impression* 1982

*Revised and rewritten by*
*M. G. Dawson-Bellone (Dott.Lett., Milan)*

PRINTED IN GREAT BRITAIN BY THE ANCHOR PRESS LTD
AND BOUND BY WM BRENDON & SON LTD
BOTH OF TIPTREE, ESSEX

# PREFACE

In preparing Part I of this Grammar, we have assumed that the reader wants to learn Italian from a practical angle and have accordingly set out those rules that will be of most use to him in this respect. The order in which they are given also takes the need for rapid progress into consideration. This order is combined with exercises containing sentences of as practical a nature as is possible within the limitations of the concurrent vocabulary, so that you will be able to put your knowledge of the language to use at an early stage. The verbs have been simplified as much as possible; for detailed reference (complete conjugation tables and so forth) we recommend our "Italian Verbs Simplified". The Hugo system of Imitated Pronunciation makes everything so much easier for the absolute beginner, as do our cassettes and disc recordings of this book.

In Part II we progress to the use of idiom and common colloquial expressions, and then to reading practice. Any serious student of the language will need to have a thorough grasp of such things, and the less dedicated will find that the business of language learning takes on a new (and much brighter) light when the living idiomatic language is displayed.

Part III consists of the answers to the grammar exercises in Part I. To begin with, you may prefer to check each sentence individually, despite the risk of glimpsing in advance the answer to the following one. This is preferable to making the same mistake unchecked throughout the whole exercise.

# CONTENTS

## PART I

## PART II

## PART III

4

# ITALIAN IN THREE MONTHS

## I

### GRAMMAR SIMPLIFIED
### EXERCISES AND VOCABULARIES
### CONVERSATION

# INTRODUCTION

The following pages contain rules on pronunciation with which you are advised to make yourself familiar before starting the first lesson. There is no need to learn these rules by heart at this stage; by referring back to them at frequent intervals you will soon know them well. For a while the imitated pronunciation of each new word is given as it is introduced into your vocabulary (see end of Lesson Nine).

In studying the lessons, first read each rule carefully, comparing with the examples underneath. Then translate and re-translate (preferably in writing) the exercise which follows, until you can put every sentence readily and correctly into Italian. The conversational sentences should be read aloud and their construction carefully noted. As the book progresses, so do these sentences become more advanced, introducing idioms and words commonly used in colloquial Italian.

# PRONUNCIATION

The stress in Italian is usually on the last but one syllable; thus **animale** is pronounced an-ne-máhl-leh, **programma** is proh-grám-mah, and **treno** is tréh-noh. Take this to be the general rule.

In some words the *final* vowel is stressed; this is always shown in printed or written Italian by a grave accent (`) placed over it: **fedeltà** is pronounced feh-del-tàh.

An important exception to the general rule is in the third person plural of verbs, where (apart from in the future tense) the stress is invariably on the last syllable but *two*—as in **mandano**, máhn-dah-no.

Sometimes the stress falls neither on the last syllable nor on the last but one; these words must be learned gradually, as they are not shown by an accent in written Italian.

In our Imitated Pronunciation the stressed syllable is marked by an acute accent (′) **only** where it deviates from the general rule. Read each syllable slowly and distinctly, as if it formed part of an English word, and your pronunciation should be good enough for all practical purposes. By using the book together with our cassette tape recordings of the text, you will of course achieve far better results.

**The Italian Alphabet** does not include the letters J, K, W, X or Y. H is little used; except as an initial letter in the words **ho, hai, ha** and **hanno** (to differentiate between **o, ai, a** and **anno**), it only appears in the combinations **ch** and **gh**.

A, ah  B, bee  C, chee  D, dee  E, ee  F, eff-eh  G, jee  H, ahk-kah
I, ee  L, ell-eh  M, em-meh  N, en-neh  O, o  P, pee  Q, koo
R, airr-reh  S, es-seh  T, tee  U, oo  V, voo  Z, dzeh-tah

**Vowels:** a is pronounced like 'ah', e like 'eh', i like 'ee', o like 'oh' and u like 'oo'.

Practically each vowel has only one sound in Italian. This is usually pronounced long, but is naturally shortened (as in other languages) by the stress falling on another syllable, or by two or more consonants following. Unless accented, e and i are pronounced slightly shorter when they are the last letter of a word.

A distinction is sometimes made between the so-called 'close' and 'open' sounds of e and o. We advise you not to trouble about this feature of pronunciation. The distinction is not often made by Italians themselves, and is not always perceptible to English ears. At any rate, the difference of sound is not indicated in writing except in a few cases where the type of sound is set by the grammar: 'close' e in **vendé** (ven-déh—the past definite of the second conjugation); 'open' o in **parlerò** etc. (parr-leh-ròh —first person singular in the future of all conjugations). To these can be added a small group of conjunctions in which the final vowel is stressed—but marked by an acute accent ('): -ché, pronounced -kéh, as in **perché, poiché, affinché, benché, finché, giacché.**

**Diphthongs:** Each vowel is pronounced separately, but if two occur together, and one of them is i or u, the two consecutive vowels form part of the *same syllable*, a, e and o being usually more stressed than the i or u.

pieno, pe'eh-no; uomo, oo'o-mo; guanto, goo'ahn-to; miei, me'eh-e; giorno, je'or-no *or* jor-no.

**Consonants:** These are pronounced as in English, with the following exceptions:

**ch** is pronounced like 'ch' in 'character':

che, keh; chi, kee; chetare, keh-tah-reh; perché, pehr-kéh.

9

**c** before **e** or **i** is pronounced like 'ch' in 'chop':

ce, cheh; ci, chee; ciarlatano*, che'ar-lah-tah-no; infelice, in-feh-lee-cheh; *but* carico, káh-re-ko.

**sc** before **e** or **i** is pronounced like 'sh' in 'shop':

scena, sheh-nah; scimmia, sheem-me'ah; uscire, oo-shee-reh; conoscimento, ko-no-she-men-to; *but* scolaro, sko-lah-ro.

**ġ** before **e** or **i** is pronounced like 'g' in 'gem':

geniale, jeh-ne-ah-leh; già*, je'áh; giuramento*, je'oo-rah-men-to; diligente, de-le-jen-teh; *but* gregario, greh-gah-re'o.

*But* when **e** or **i** does not follow, **c** and **ġ** are pronounced hard, as in 'coat' and 'go'.

**ġh** is pronounced like 'g' in 'go':

ghermire, gairr-mee-reh; ghirlanda, gheerr-lahn-dah; spighe, spee-geh.

**h** is not pronounced at all:

ho, o; hai, ah'e; ha, ah; hanno, ahn-no.

**qu** is pronounced like 'qu' in 'queen':

quale, kwah-leh; qui, kwee; questo, kwess-to; conquista, kon-kwiss-tah.

**s** is sharp, like 'ss', at the beginning of a word; but between two vowels it is generally pronounced like 'z':

chiesa, ke'eh-zah; desiderare, deh-zee-deh-rah-reh; scusare, skoo-zah-reh; *but* senso, sen-so; solo, so-lo.

**z** is pronounced like 'ts', but is softer (like 'dz') at the beginning of a few unimportant words:

pranzo, prahn-tso; zia, tsee-ah; scienza, she'en-tsah; zero, dzeh-ro.

No rule can be given showing exactly when **s** and **z** are pronounced hard (like 'ss' and 'ts'), and when soft (like 'z' and 'dz'). This difference must be mastered gradually, by practice and observation. It may be as well to point out, however, that **s** is sharp in the middle of words formed by combining two others, as in **stasera**—an abbreviation of **questa sera**; this **s** is really the first letter of **sera**.

---

* When **ci** or **ġi** comes before **a**, **o** or **u**, the **i** is hardly heard, if at all; but its presence is necessary, to make the **c** or **ġ** soft. These three words could therefore be imitated equally well as char-lah-tah-no, jah, joo-rah-men-to. Without the **i**, the pronunciation would be car-lah-tah-no, gah, goo-rah-men-to.

10

An initial **s** followed immediately by a consonant is called by Italians 's impura' (impure **s**), and is usually pronounced like 'ss': **spedire**, speh-dee-reh. But **s** is made softer before **b, d, ǵ, l, m, n, r** and **v**, approaching the English 'z' sound. For example, **svelto** sounds more like zvell-to than svell-to.

**Double consonants:** When a consonant is doubled, it is almost pronounced twice. That is to say, it must be lingered on, and pronounced more slowly, more markedly and more drawn out. **zz** is generally hard, like 'ts', but in some words it is soft, like 'dz'. As with the hard and soft **s**, no rule can be given to show in which words **zz** has the hard sound, and in which the soft sound. Examples follow:

classe, klahss-seh; città, chit-táh; piccolo, peek-ko-lo; fiamma, fe'ahm-mah; braccio, braht-cho; maggiore, mahd-jor-reh; anno, ahn-no; occupare, ok-koo-pah-reh; obbligato, ob-ble-gah-to; bellezza, bel-let-tsah; mezzo, med-dzo.

**Liquid sounds:** These have no exact equivalent in English. Pronounce them according to our imitation, which is a very near approximation to the actual sound, and you will always be understood.

**ǵl** before **i** sounds very similar to 'lli' in 'million'.

gli, l'yee; luglio, loo-l'yo; egli, eh-l'ye; sbaglio, zbah-l'yo.

**ǵn** before any vowel sounds very similar to 'ni' in 'union'.

ogni, o-n'ye; sdegno, zdeh-n'yo; segnare, seh-n'yah-reh; impugnano, im-poo-n'yah-no.

The combination **ǵl** and **ǵn** are really a compound consonant rather than two separate consonants. Both belong to the same syllable as the vowel which follows, for which reason **egli, oǵni,** etc., are imitated more correctly and exactly as shown although a simplification might be ehl-ye, ohn-ye etc. In a few unimportant words, **ǵl** is not liquid, but is pronounced as in English. For instance, **ǵlicerina, neǵligenza** are pronounced gle-cheh-ree-nah, neh-gle-jen-tsah.

11

# LESSON ONE

**1.** THE INDEFINITE ARTICLE. *A* and *an* are translated **un** before a masculine noun, **una** before a feminine noun:

> a train   **un treno** (oong treh-noh)
> a star   **una stella** (oo-nah stehl-lah)

Before a word commencing with a vowel, **una** is written **un'**, whereas **un** becomes **uno** before z or st, sp, sc, sm, sn, sq:

> an idea   **un' idea** (ee-deh-ah)
> a pupil (*f*)   **un' allieva** (al-li-eh-vah)
> a zero   **uno zero** (dseh-roh)
> a mistake   **uno sbaglio** (zbah-l'yeo)

## EXERCISE I

1 a pupil (*m*);  2 a person;  3 a station;  4 an arrival;  5 an explosion;  6 a road;  7 a place;  8 a swing;  9 a stick;  10 a grass.

VOCABULARY: person, **persona** *f* (pehr-soh-nah); station, **stazione** *f* (stah-tsi-oh-neh); arrival, **arrivo** *m* (ar-ree-voh); explosion, **scoppio** *m* (scop-pe'o); road, **strada** *f* (strah-dah); place, **posto** *m* (pos-toh); swing, **altalena** *f* (ahl-tah-leh-nah); stick, **stecco** *m* (stehk-koh); grass, **erba** *f* (ehr-bah).

**2.** THE PLURAL/SINGULAR PATTERN. We have already seen how masculine nouns end in **-o** and feminine nouns end in **-a**. A third ending, in **-e**, may belong to both genders, and a few masculine nouns end in **-a**.

> a portion   **una porzione** (por-tsi-oh-neh)
> an order   **un órdine** (ór-de-neh)
> a programme   **un programma** (proh-gram-mah)
> an athlete   **un, un' atleta** (aht-leh-tah)

The plural is not formed—as in English—by adding **s** to the singular; apart from a few exceptions (see Appendix) masculine endings change into **-i**, and feminine endings change into **-e** or **-i**, according to this pattern:

*m* **treni** (treh-nee) .. *f* **stelle** (stehl-eh)
*m* **ordini** (ór-de-nee)  *f* **porzioni** (por-tsi-oh-nee)
*m* **programmi** (proh-gram-mee)

## EXERCISE II

1 arrivals;  2 two roads;  3 a sign;  4 places;  5 two
stations;  6 a place;  7 ten minutes;  8 a minute;  9 a coffee;
10 two coffees;  11 a (cup of) tea.

VOCABULARY: two, **due** (doo-eh); sign, **cartello** *m* (carr-tel-loh); ten
minutes, **dieci minuti** *m* (dee-eh-tchee mee-noo-tee); coffee, **caffè** *m*
*s & pl* (kahf-féh); tea (drink), **tè** *m s & pl* (teh).

N.B. The only stresses to be written in Italian are those on
the last syllable: caffè, perché (*why*). However, in this book you
will find that the stress is indicated the first time a word is used,
if the stress should be on the third or fourth syllable.

**3.**               Present tense of AVERE (*to have*)

| I have | **io ho** (ee-o oh) |
| you have ('thou') | **tu hai** (too ah'e) |
| he has | **ha** (ah) |
| we have | **noi abbiamo** (no-ee ahb-be-ah-mo) |
| you have | **voi avete** (vo-ee ah-veh-teh) |
| they have | **hanno** (ahn-no) |

The second person singular of a verb (**tu**) is used in most
cases where in English we would use Christian names. The
plural form (**voi**) can also be used in more formal cases. In this
book, where we put (*fam*) against 'you', use the singular (familiar)
form.

13

4. **SUBJECT PRONOUNS.** Verbs are seldom accompanied by the subject pronoun (*I*, *you*, *we*, etc) in Italian, the verbal form being sufficiently characterised in each case. You have just learnt **io**, **tu**, **noi** and **voi**. The remaining pronouns are shown below:

| | |
|---|---|
| he | **lui** (loo-ee); **egli** (eh-l'ye) |
| she | **lei** (leh-ee); **essa** (ess-sah), **ella** (ell-lah) |
| it | **esso** (ess-so) |
| they | **loro** (lor-oh); **essi** (ess-ee), **esse** (ess-eh) |

When to use which? **Lui**, **lei** and **loro** are the most used, at least in spoken language; the others belong nowadays to rather formal discourse, written or not. *It* is only exceptionally translated, consequently **esso** is seldom used.

5. **NOT** is translated by **non** (pronounced as in English), which is placed before the verb:

| | |
|---|---|
| I have not | **io non ho** |
| Frank has not | **Franco non ha** |

Remember that the initial **h** is never sounded in Italian.

### EXERCISE III

1 io ho;  2 non ho;  3 esse non hanno;  4 avete?  5 essi hanno;  6 non avete?  7 tu non hai;  8 you have;  9 they have not;  10 have we?  11 have we not?  12 he has.

14

# CONVERSATION

| | |
|---|---|
| Chi[1] non ha posto? | Who has not got a place? |
| Ecco[2] un posto. | Here is a place. |
| Dov'è[3] la stazione. | Where is the station? |
| Eccola.[4] | There it is. |
| Abbiamo tempo[5] per[6] un caffè? | Have we got time for a coffee? |
| Avete dieci minuti. | You have ten minutes. |
| Hai freddo[7]? | Are you cold? |
| No[8], sto[9] bene[10], grazie[11]. | No thank you, I am alright. |
| Avete visto[12] il cartello[13]? | Have you seen the sign? |
| Quale[14] cartello? | Which sign? |

PRONUNCIATION: 1 kee; 2 eh-ko; 3 dohv (doh-veh when apostrophe is not used); 4 éh-koh-lah; 5 tem-poh; 6 pehr; 7 frehd-doh; 8 noh; 9 stoh; 10 ben-neh; 11 grah-tse-eh; 12 vee-sto; 13 carr-tel-loh; 14 kwah-leh.

# LESSON TWO

**6.** THE is translated **il** before a masculine singular noun and **la** before a feminine singular noun, when these begin with a consonant. With nouns beginning with a vowel, **l'** is used:

| the teacher | **il maestro** (eel mah-ess-troh) |
|---|---|
| the order | **l'ordine** (lór-de-neh) |
| the hall | **la sala** (lah sah-lah) |
| the guest | **l'invitata** (leen-vee-tah-tah) |

**Lo** must be used instead of **il** before masculine singular nouns beginning with **z**, impure **s** and **ġn**:

| the student | **lo studente** (loh stoo-den-teh) |
|---|---|
| the uncle | **lo zio** (loh tsee-oh) |
| the dumpling | **lo ġnocco** (loh n'yok-koh) |

15

**7.** THE in the plural is translated **i** (ee), **le** (leh) and **ġli** (l'yee). See how these are used with the same nouns as shown above:

| | |
|---|---|
| the teachers | **i maestri** |
| the orders | **ġli ordini** |
| ~~the halls~~ | ~~le sale~~ |
| the guests *f* | **le invitate** |
| the guests *m* | **ġli, ġl'invitati** |
| the students | **ġli studenti** |
| the uncles | **ġli zìi** |
| the dumplings | **ġli, ġnocchi** |

## EXERCISE I

1 the father, the fathers; 2 a sister, the sisters; 3 the mother, the mothers; 4 a brother, the brothers; 5 the flat, the flats; 6 the space, the spaces; 7 the stairs; 8 an acrobat, the acrobats; 9 the knapsack, the knapsacks; 10 the Englishman, the Englishmen.

VOCABULARY: father, **padre** (pah-dreh); sister, **sorella** (soh-rel-lah); mother, **madre** (mah-dreh); brother, **fratello** (frah-tel-loh); a flat, **appartamento** (ahp-par-tah-men-toh); space, **spazio** (spah-tse'o); stairs, **scale** *f* (skah-leh); acrobat, **acróbata** *m/f* (ah-kró-bah-tah); knapsack, **zàino** *m* (tsáh-e-noh); Englishman, **inġlese** (in-gleh-zeh).

**8.**  Present tense of ESSERE (*to be*)

| | |
|---|---|
| I am | **sono** (soh-noh) |
| you (*fam*) are | **sei** (seh-e) |
| he, she, it is | **è** (eh) |
| we are | **siamo** (see-ah-moh) |
| you are | **siete** (see-eh-teh) |
| they are | **sono** (soh-noh) |

## EXERCISE II

1 she is the sister; 2 they are the guests; 3 are you Franco? 4 we are brother and sister; 5 am I late? 6 you are students.

VOCABULARY: late, **in ritardo** (ree-tahr-doh).

**9.** **PREPOSITIONS.** The main prepositions are:

| | | | | |
|---|---|---|---|---|
| of | **di** (de) | by, from | **da** (dah) |
| to | **a** (ah) | for | **per** (pehr) |
| in | **in** (een) | with | **con** (con) |
| on | **su** (soo) | | |

These prepositions are used in the same way as in English, before the indefinite article (a):

| | |
|---|---|
| with a portion | **con una porzione** |
| to a pupil | **a un allievo** |

**10.** However, with the definite article (*the*) they are joined and form one word (contracted prepositions):

| | |
|---|---|
| in the flat | **nell'appartamento** |
| from the station | **dalla stazione** |

Contractions occur regularly with the above prepositions (except with per and con—whose contracted forms have become obsolete). The following table will show clearly all possible forms of contracted prepositions:

**11.**

| | il | la | l' | lo | i | le | gli |
|---|---|---|---|---|---|---|---|
| **di** | del | della | dell' | dello | dei | delle | degli |
| **a** | al | alla | all' | allo | ai | alle | agli |
| **in** | nel | nella | nell' | nello | nei | nelle | negl¡ |
| **su** | sul | sulla | sull' | sulle | sui | sulle | sugli |
| **da** | dal | dalla | dall' | dalle | dai | dalle | dagli |
| **con** | col | con la | coll' | con lo | coi | con le | con gli |

17

**12.** POSSESSION. Since in Italian there is no equivalent of the English *'s* (e.g. *the girl's costume*), possession is expressed by **di, del**, etc.

| the teacher's book | **il libro del maestro** |
| Anna's brother | **il fratello di Anna** |

Notice that the preposition is also used in phrases such as:

| **la porta della cucina** | the kitchen door |
| **la stazione di Dover** | Dover station |

## EXERCISE III

1 coffee for two, please;  2 on the chair;  3 the door of the apartment;  4 in the times of the Romans;  5 Ann is in the kitchen;  6 on the road.

VOCABULARY: for two, **per due**; please, **per piacere** (pe'ah-cheh-reh); chair, **sedia** *f* (seh-de'ah); door, **porta** (porr-tah); in the times, **al tempo** *m* (tem-poh); Romans, **romani** *m* (ro-mah-nee); in the kitchen, **in cucina** (koo-chee-nah).

## CONVERSATIONAL SENTENCES

| Chi siete? | Who are you? |
| Siamo gli allievi del maestro Martelli[1]. | We are Mr. Martelli's pupils (*literally :* teacher Martelli's . . .) |
| Quanti[2] appartamenti ci sono in questa[3] casa? | How many flats are there in this house? |
| Tre[4]: uno per una persona sola[5], due per delle famiglie[6]. | Three: one for one person, two for families. |
| A che[7] piano[8] è l'appartamento dei Martelli? | What floor is the Martelli's flat on? |
| Al secondo, credo[9]. | Second floor, I think. |

PRONUNCIATION: 1 marr-tell-ee; 2 quant-ee; 3 ques-tah; 4 treh; 5 soh-lah; 6 fah-mee-l'yeh; 7 keh; 8 pe-ah-no; 9 creh-doh.

# LESSON THREE

**13.** AND, OR and YES are translated **e**, **o** and **si**; before words beginning with a vowel, **e** becomes **ed**—especially before e- and a-. The expansion **o** to **od** is infrequent, whereas the preposition **a** normally becomes **ad**:

| | |
|---|---|
| and he said . . . | **ed egli disse** . . . |
| to Ann and to us | **ad Anna e a noi** |
| two or one | **due o uno** |

**14.** POSSESSIVE ADJECTIVES. A brief explanation of the difference between these and possessive pronouns may be helpful: adjectives are always followed by a noun, whereas pronouns are used instead of a noun. In both cases they take the same gender and number as the noun (but see **loro** below). See also §19 and §20.

| | |
|---|---|
| our | **nostro, nostra, nostri, nostre** |
| your | **vostro, vostra, vostri, vostre** |
| their | **loro** |

PRONUNCIATION: nos-troh, -trah, -tree, -treh; vos-troh, -tree, -trah, -treh; loh-roh.

Unlike the other possessive adjectives, **loro** does not vary at all, nor does it omit the article with words that indicate (in the singular) a near relation:

| | |
|---|---|
| our train | **il nostro treno** |
| your sister | **vostra sorella** |
| their brother | **il loro fratello** |
| their houses | **le loro case** |

## EXERCISE I

1 our mother;  2 your relations;  3 their arrival;  4 our programmes;  5 your uncle is young, their aunt is young;  6 one by one;  7 either one or the other;  8 their coffees.

VOCABULARY: relations, **parenti** (pah-ren-tee); young, **gióvane** (jóh-vah-neh); aunt, **zía** *f* (tsee-ah); one, **uno**; either . . . or, **o . . . o**; other, **altro** (ahl-troh).

19

**15.** QUALIFYING ADJECTIVES agree in gender and number with the noun they qualify and generally follow that noun, thus:

| | |
|---|---|
| an Italian book | **un libro italiano** |
| three easy rules | **tre régole fácili** |

**16.** PLURAL OF ADJECTIVES. This is formed in the same way as the plural of nouns, see §7.

The feminine of adjectives is formed by changing the masculine ending **-o** into **-a**; those ending in **-e** do not change.

| | |
|---|---|
| a modern flat | **un appartamento moderno** (moh-der-noh) |
| a modern house | **una casa moderna** |
| a kind sister | **una sorella gentile** (gen-tee-leh) |
| a kind uncle | **uno zio gentile** |
| some kind relations | **dei parenti gentili** |
| modern houses | **le case moderne** |

## EXERCISE II

1 the new page;   2 a yellow flower;   3 cold winds;   4 the young teachers (*f*);   5 our journey is short;   6 your chairs are narrow;   7 the stars are bright;   8 a loud bang;   9 two fat sisters;   10 a thick book.

VOCABULARY: new, **nuovo/a** (noo'o-voh/ah); page, **página** *f* (páh-jee-nah); yellow, **giallo** (jal-loh); flower, **fiore** *m* (fee'o-reh); wind, **vento** *m* (ven'-toh); journey, **viaggio** *m* (ve'ah-djoh); short, **corto** (corr-toh); narrow, **stretto** (streh-ttoh); bright, **lucente** (loo-chen-teh); loud, **forte** (forr-teh); bang, **colpo** *m* (col-poh); fat, **grasso** (gra-ssoh); thick, **spesso** (speh-ssoh).

**17.** THE FIRST CONJUGATION. This consists of all those Italian verbs with infinitive ending in **-are**. There are two more conjugations, with infinitives ending in **-ere** and **-ire**; they do not account for many verbs, and will be dealt with later. The part of the infinitive preceding the ending is called the stem:

| INFINITIVE | STEM |
|---|---|
| **parlare** (par-lah-reh) | **parl-** |
| **ascoltare** (ah-skol-tah-reh) | **ascolt-** |
| **trovare** (troh-vah-reh) | **trov-** |

**18.** PRESENT TENSE of verbs ending in **-are**. This is formed by adding to the stem the endings printed in bold type below (subject pronouns will no longer be indicated):

| I speak | parl**o** (par-loh) |
|---|---|
| you speak (*fam*) | parl**i** (par-lee) |
| he, she, it speaks | parl**a** (par-lah) |
| we speak | parl**iamo** (par-lee'ah-moh) |
| you speak | parl**ate** (par-lah-teh) |
| they speak | párl**ano** (pár-lah-noh) |

In the 3rd person plural the stress is on the stem, not on the ending, and generally on the third but last syllable. This rule applies to the three conjugations. We print it here simply as a reminder; it is not normally shown in Italian.

## EXERCISE III

1 we find that . . .;   2 you (*fam*) listen a lot;   3 you speak well;   4 if I invite the Martellis;   5 they accept;   6 time passes quickly;   7 we listen together;   8 you (*fam*) accept.

VOCABULARY: that, **che** (keh); a lot, **molto** (mohl-toh); well, **bene** (beh-neh); if, **se** (seh); to invite, **invitare** (in-vee-tar-eh); to accept, **accettare** (a-chet-tah-reh); time, **tempo** *m* (tem-poh); to pass, **passare** (pass-ah-reh); quickly, **in fretta** (in freh-ttah); together, **insieme** (in-see-eh-meh).

## CONVERSATION

| | |
|---|---|
| Pronto[1] ! | Hallo! |
| Pronto! Chi parla? | Hallo! Who is speaking? |
| Qui[2] è Franco[3] Brilli[4], un amico[5] di Bruno[6]. E' in casa, Bruno? | This is Franco Brilli speaking, a friend of Bruno's. Is Bruno there? |
| Sì, lo chiamo[7] súbito[8]. | Yes, I'll call him. |
| Grazie. | Thank you. |
| Pronto, Franco? | Hallo, Franco? |

| | |
|---|---|
| Ciao, Bruno. Finalmente[9] ti trovo in casa. Desídero[10] parlare con te di una cosa importante[11]. Va bene, vengo[12] a casa tua[13]. | Hallo, Bruno. At last I've found you at home! I'd like to speak to you about something important. All right, I'll come round to your place. |

Notice how the Italian Present tense translates not only the English simple Present but often the Present Continuous, the Future and the Perfect. See also §34 and §36.

PRONUNCIATION: 1 pron-toh; 2 quee; 3 fran-coh; 4 bree-llee; 5 ah-mee-coh; 6 broo-noh; 7 kee'a-moh; 8 soó-bee-toh; 9 fee-nal-men-teh; 10 deh-seé-der-oh; 11 im-porr-tan-teh; 12 ven-goh; 13 too-ah.

# LESSON FOUR

**19. POSSESSIVE ADJECTIVES**

| | |
|---|---|
| my | **mio, mia, miéi, mie** |
| your (*fam*) | **tuo, tua, tuói, tue** |
| his, her, its | **suo, sua, suói, sue** |

PRONUNCIATION: mee-oh, mee-ah, me'éh-ee, mee-eh; too-oh, too-ah, to'óh-ee, too-eh; soo-oh, soo-ah, soo'oh-ee, soo-eh.

It is important to remember that (with the exception of **loro**, §14) these possessive adjectives always take the gender of the following noun. Such a point can easily be forgotten when a feminine noun is prefaced by 'his'—the temptation is to put the masculine form of adjective. Note also that the article is omitted when the possessive adjective is followed by a word indicating a close relation in the singular.

| | |
|---|---|
| your daughter | **tua figlia** (fee-l'ya) |
| my sons | **i miei figli** |
| her, his car | **la sua mácchina** (mác-kee-nah) |
| her, his books | **i suoi libri** |

**20. POSSESSIVE PRONOUNS.** *mine, yours, ours* etc., are translated **mio, tuo, nostro**, etc., being the same words as shown in §14 and §19 as possessive adjectives.

22

| Whose flat is this? Ours. | **Di chi e questo appartamento? Nostro.** |
| These letters are yours. | **Queste léttere sono tue.** (queh-steh léh-tteh-reh) |
| His/her tea is stronger than mine. | **Il suo tè è più forte del mio.** (pe'óoh) |

The article is usually used with possessive pronouns after the verb **essere**, and omitted with adjectives. ✓

## EXERCISE I

1 my letters; 2 your newspaper; 3 his/her uncles; 4 your books and mine; 5 their flat and yours; 6 your daughter and my grand-daughters; 7 I buy my post-cards, he buys his; 8 which is more comfortable, your seat or hers/his?; 9 a friend of his lives here; 10 sometimes I meet two pupils of yours.

VOCABULARY: newspaper, **giornale** *m* (jor-nah-leh); grand-daughter, **nipote** (nee-poh-teh); postcard, **cartolina** *f* (car-toh-lee-nah); to buy, **comprare**; comfortable, **cómodo** (cóh-moh-doh); seat, **posto** *m*; to live, **abitare**, **vívere** (ah-bee-tah-reh, veé-veh-reh); friend, **amico**, **amica** (ah-mee-coh); to meet, **incontrare** (in-con-trah-reh); sometimes, **a volte** (vol-teh).

**21.** DO NOT is translated **non** (see also §4).

| They do not wish | **Non desíderano** |
| She does not always accept | **Non accetta sempre** (or: **Non sempre accetta**) |

**22.** DO, DOES, DID in the Interrogative form are never translated in Italian. Generally, no change in word-order is made in Italian when asking a question; there is merely a raising intonation when speaking and the addition of a question mark in writing.

| Does he speak English? | **Parla inglese?** |
| Do they invite your friend to their parties? | **Invitano il vostro amico ai loro ricevimenti?** (ree-che-vee-men-tee) |
| Have you got two cars? | **Avete due mácchine?** |
| *but:* Are these knives yours? | **Sono vostri questi coltelli?** (col-teh-llee) |
| Is the big parcel mine? | **E' mio il pacco grande?** (pac-koh gran-deh) |

## EXERCISE II

1 is he very ill?;　2 have we time to buy a newspaper?;
3 have you a photo of Gianni?;　4 when do your parents arrive?;
5 do you go on holiday together?;　6 is supper ready?

VOCABULARY: very, **molto**; ill, **ammalato** (ah-ma-lah-toh); photo,
**foto** *f* (foh-toh); Gianni (Jan-nee); to arrive, **arrivare** (ar-ree-vah-reh);
parents, **genitori** *m* (jeh-nee-tor-ee); holiday, **vacanza** *f* (vah-can-tsa);
together, **insieme** (in-si-eh-meh); supper, **cena** *f* (chay-nah); ready,
**pronto**.

**23.**　Whereas in English there is only one form of address, in
Italian there are two, a familiar form and a polite one. With
friends, relatives, colleagues and children the familiar **tu**
and **voi** are used. With acquaintances, elders and betters,
**Lei** is used in the singular. In the plural, the corresponding
form **Loro** often gives way nowadays to **voi**, which is also
used in addressing meetings or speaking to an audience.

　　The capital L is used by Italians only in correspondence.
In this book, however, it will be used to mark the difference from **lei**, **loro** meaning *she, they*.

**24.**　With **Lei** and **Loro**, the 3rd person singular and plural of
verbs is used. Consequently, the forms for **Lei** and **Loro**
are exactly the same as those for *he, she, it* and *they*.

| | |
|---|---|
| Yes, madam, you are right. | **Sì, signora, ha ragione.** (see-n'yoh-rah, rah-joh-neh) |
| You are perfectly right, gentlemen. | **Loro hanno perfettamente ragione, signori.** |

## EXERCISE III

1 no, madam, you are wrong;　2 are you Mr. Brilli?;　3 do
you and your family live in England?;　4 he always arrives late;
5 they are having a holiday;　6 you work (polite form) too much.

VOCABULARY: to be wrong, **aver torto** (torr-toh); family, **famiglia** *f*
(fah-mee-l'yah); to have a holiday, **essere in vacanza**; to work, **lavorare**
(lah-voh-rah-reh); too much, **troppo**.

# CONVERSATION

| | |
|---|---|
| Buongiorno[1], signore. Che cosa desídera? | Good morning, sir. What would you like? |
| Una bottiglia[2] di vino[3] rosso[4] di buona[5] qualità[6]. | A bottle of good red wine. |
| Va bene questo Chianti[7] Bellini[8] a 900[9] lire[10]? | What about this nine hundred lire bottle of Chianti Bellini? |
| Sì, va bene. Mi dia[11] anche[12] un baráttolo[13] di olive[14] e un pacchetto[15] di biscotti[16] salati[17], per piacere. | Yes, all right, and please give me a jar of olives and a packet of salted biscuits. |
| Ecco, signore. Desidera altro? | There you are, sir. Anything else? |
| No, grazie. Quanto[18] fa[19] in tutto[20]? | No, thank you. How much is that altogether? |
| Milleottocento[21] lire. | One thousand eight hundred lire. |
| Ecco a lei. | There you are. |
| Grazie, signore, arrivederla[22]! | Thank you, sir. Good bye. |

PRONUNCIATION: 1 boo-on-jorr-no; 2 bot-tee-l'ya; 3 vee-no; 4 roh-ssoh; 5 boo-o-nah; 6 quah-lee-taàh; 7 kee-an-tee; 8 beh-llee-nee; 9 noh-veh-chen-toh; 10 lee-reh; 11 dee-ah; 12 an-keh; 13 bah-rát-toh-loh; 14 oh-lee-veh; 15 pac-keh-ttoh; 16 bis-coh-ttee; 17 sah-lah-tee; 18 quan-toh; 19 fah; 20 too-ttoh; 21 mil-leh-otto-chen-toh; 22 ahree-veh-der-lah.

25

# LESSON FIVE

**25.** THE SECOND CONJUGATION. This consists of verbs ending in **-ere**. Not many of them are regular; those which are include:

| INFINITIVE | STEM |
|---|---|
| crédere (créh-deh-reh) | créd- |
| temere (teh-meh-reh) | tem- |
| pérdere (pérr-deh-reh) | pérd- |

**26.** PRESENT TENSE of regular **-ere** verbs:

| | |
|---|---|
| I believe | **credo** (creh-doh) |
| you believe (*fam*) | **credi** (creh-dee) |
| he, she, it believes | **crede** (cred-deh) |
| we believe | **crediamo** (creh-dee-ah-moh) |
| you believe | **credete** (creh-deteh) |
| they believe | **crédono** (créh-doh-noh) |

## EXERCISE I

1 I don't believe (and: I don't think so); 2 do you think so?; 3 I think that . . .; 4 children believe in Father Christmas; 5 Ann believes anything; 6 believe me . . .

VOCABULARY: children, **bambini** *m* (bam-bee-nee); Father Christmas, **Babbo Natale** (bah-bboh nat-ah-leh); anything, **tutto**; me, **a me** (meh).

**27.** SOME, ANY meaning 'a certain amount of' or 'a number' are translated thus:

| | |
|---|---|
| Have you any matches? | **Hai dei fiammíferi ?** (fee-ahm-meé-fer-ee) |
| He buys some magazines. | **Compra delle riviste.** (re-vis-teh) |
| Buy some wine! | **Comprate del vino!** |
| Do you bring any good news? | **Porti buone notizie ?** (porr-tee, no-teet-se'eh) |

Sometimes *some* and *any* are omitted. See also §82.

26

**28.** Adverbs of manner (e.g. *readily*) are formed in Italian by adding **-mente** to the feminine adjective:

| | |
|---|---|
| divinely | **divinamente** (de-ve-nah-men-teh) |
| humanely | **umanamente** (oo-mah-nah-men-teh) |
| ordinarily | **ordinariamente** (orr-dee-nah-re-ah-men-teh) |

Notice the dropping of the final **-e** following r, o, l:

| | |
|---|---|
| easily | **facilmente** (fah-cheel-men-teh) |
| regularly | **regolarmente** (reh-go-larr-men-teh) |

These adverbs generally follow the verb but they go in front of adjectives.

## EXERCISE II

1 I write slowly in Italian;  2 Anna and Carlo send postcards regularly;  3 he is quietly waiting to begin;  4 the village shop is extraordinarily well-stocked;  5 the library is normally open.

VOCABULARY: to write, **scrívere** (screé-veh-reh); slow, **lento**; to send, **mandare** (mahn-dah-reh); to wait, **aspettare** (ass-peht-tar-eh); quiet, **tranquillo** (trahn-queel-loh); to begin, **cominciare** (com-in-char-eh); village, **villaggio** *m* (vil-lah-jjo); shop, **negozio** *m* (neh-goh-ts'io); extraordinary, **straordinario** (strah-or-de-nah-re'o); well-stocked, **ben fornito** (for-neeh-to); library, **biblioteca** *f* (be-ble'o-teh-cah); normal, **normale** (norr-mah-leh); open, **aperto** (ah-pair-to).

**29.** THERE IS, THERE ARE are translated **c'è, ci sono**:

| | |
|---|---|
| There is a letter from Ann. | **C'è una lettera di Anna.** |
| There are little boys and girls. | **Ci sono bambini e bambine.** |
| Is Gianni there? | **C'è Gianni?** |
| No, he isn't there. | **No, non c'è.** |

**30.** CARDINAL NUMBERS, 1 to 20

| | |
|---|---|
| 1 uno, una | 11 úndici (oón-dee-chee) |
| 2 due | 12 dódici (dóh-dee-chee) |
| 3 tre (treh) | 13 trédici (tréh-dee-chee) |
| 4 quattro (kwah-troh) | 14 quattórdici (quat-tór-dee-chee) |
| 5 cinque (chin-queh) | 15 quíndici (quín-dee-chee) |
| 6 sei (seh-ee) | 16 sédici (séh-dee-chee) |
| 7 sette (seh-tteh) | 17 diciassette (de-cha-sseh-tteh) |
| 8 otto (oh-ttoh) | 18 diciotto (de-chot-toh) |
| 9 nove (noh-veh) | 19 diciannove (de-chan-nov-eh) |
| 10 dieci (de'eh-chee) | 20 venti (ven-tee) |

## EXERCISE III

1 there is a cloud in the sky;  2 there are boats in the sea; 3 there is one difficulty;  4 are there any strawberries in the garden?;  5 there are presents and presents;  6 there's time; 7 there is a surprise for you;  8 there are two gentlemen in your office (*polite*).

VOCABULARY: cloud, **núvola** *f* (nóo-voh-lah); sky, **cielo** *m* (che-loh); boats, **barca** *f* (barr-cah, *pl.* barr-keh); sea, **mare** *m* (mah-reh); difficulty **difficoltà** *f* (de-fe-coll-táh); strawberry, **frágola** *f* (fráh-go-lah); garden, **giardino** *m* (jarr-dee-noh); present, **regalo** *m* (reh-ga-loh); surprise, **sorpresa** *f* (sorr-preh-sah); office, **ufficio** *m* (oo-ffee-cho).

## CONVERSATION

| | |
|---|---|
| Che ora è? | What time is it? |
| E' quasi mezzogiorno! | It is nearly midday. |
| A che ora sono arrivato qui? | At what time did I get here? |
| Alle nove e un quarto[2]. | At a quarter past nine. |
| Allora sono due ore e mezzo che lavoro. | I have been working two hours and a half then. |
| Quando vuoi[3] uscire[4]? | When do you want to go out? |
| Adesso[5] teléfono[6] a un amico per pranzare[7] insieme all'una. | I am going to telephone a friend to have lunch with me at one o'clock. |
| Va bene. Torna quando vuoi, alle due e mezzo o alle tre. | All right. Come back when you want, 2.30 or 3 o'clock. |

PRONUNCIATION: 1 meh-dso-jor-no; 2 quah-rrto; 3 voo-oy; 4 oo-shee-reh; 5 ah-deh-sso; 6 teh-léh-foh-no; 7 pran-tsah-reh.

## LESSON SIX

**31.** Verbs ending in **-ire**, the Third Conjugation, divide into those that (*a*) insert **-isc-** between the stem and the endings of the Present Tense of the Indicative (and the Subjunctive) and (*b*) those that don't.

| INFINITIVE | STEM |
|---|---|
| (*a*) **capire** (cah-peer-reh) | **cap-** |
| **aġire** (ah-geer-reh) | **aġ-** |
| **tossire** (toss-eer-reh) | **toss-** |
| (*b*) **dormire** (dorr-meer-reh) | **dorm-** |
| **servire** (serr-veer-reh) | **serv-** |
| **seġuire** (seh-goo'ee-reh) | **seġu-** |

**32.** PRESENT TENSE of **-ire** verbs

(*a*)
I finish *etc.*

finisco (fin-ees-coh)
finisci (fin-ee-shee)
finisce (fin-ee-sheh)
finiamo (fin-ee-a-moh)
finite (fin-ee-teh)
finíscono (fin-eés-co-noh)

(*b*)

| | |
|---|---|
| I leave | parto (parr-toh) |
| you leave | parti (parr-tee) |
| he, she, it leaves | parte (parr-teh) |
| we leave | partiamo (parr-tee-ah-moh) |
| you leave | partite (parr-tee-teh) |
| they leave | pártono (párr-toh-noh) |

## EXERCISE I

1 they sleep;   2 they act;   3 we serve;   4 we understand;
5 do you understand?;   6 he/she doesn't understand;   7 he/she
sleeps;   8 he/she follows;   9 I understand;   10 I don't follow.

VOCABULARY: to sleep, **dormire**; to act, **aġire**; to serve, **servire**; to understand, **capire**; to follow, **seġuire**.

29

# CONVERSATION

Sai[1] contare[2] per dieci?

Can you count in tens?

Certo[3]: dieci, venti, trenta[4], quaranta, cinquanta[5], sessanta, settanta, ottanta, novanta, cento[6], centodieci . . .

Certainly: 10, 20, *etc.*, 110 . . .

Basta[7] così[8]. Sentiamo ora i numerali ordinali.

That's enough. Now let's have ordinal numbers.

Primo[9], secondo, terzo[10], quarto, quinto, sesto, séttimo, ottavo, nono, décimo[11], undicésimo, dodicésimo . . .

First, second, third, fourth, fifth, sixth, seventh, eighth, ninth, tenth, eleventh, twelfth . . .

Vedo[12] che hai capito: dall'úndici in poi gli ordinali si fórmano aggiungendo[13] -ésimo ai numeri cardinali.

I see that you have understood: from 11 onwards ordinal numbers are formed by adding -ésimo to the cardinal numbers.

Sì. E si dice[14]: la ventiquattrésima ora, il quindicésimo giorno!

Yes. And we say: the 24th hour, the 15th day!

PRONUNCIATION: 1 saee; 2 con-tah-reh; 3 cher-toh; 4 tren-tah; 5 chin-quan-tah; 6 chen-toh; 7 bass-tah; 8 co-zeé; 9 pree-moh; 10 terr-tsoh; 11 déh-cheh-moh; 12 veh-doh; 13 ahd-joon-jen-doh; 14 dee-cheh.

33.  PAST PARTICIPLES. **Parlato, creduto, finito** (spoken, believed, finished) are the Past Participles of **parlare, credere, finire.** They are formed by adding the endings **-ato, -uto, -ito** (ah-toh, oo-toh, ee-toh) to the respective Infinitive stems. They are used after the auxiliary verbs essere and avere in compound tenses.

| | |
|---|---|
| mand-are | **mandato** |
| perd-ere | **perduto** |
| dorm-ire | **dormito** |

30

**34.** PERFECT TENSE. This is the basic tense of the past in spoken Italian:

| I have found | **ho trovato** |
|---|---|
| you have finished | **hai finito** |
| he, she has had | **ha avuto** |

Later on we shall see the other Past tenses and their use. Note that the auxiliary **essere** is compounded with **essere**, like a group of verbs expressing motion:

| we have been | **siamo stati** |
|---|---|
| you have gone | **siete andati** |
| they have come | **sono venuti** |

The past participles of verbs taking **essere** have **-o, -a, -i, -e** endings depending on the gender and number of the persons or things that went, came, etc.

## EXERCISE II

1 he has sent twelve roses;  2 they have found 1000 lire; 3 I feared the worst;  4 you didn't believe me;  5 we have arrived;  6 have you understood?  7 have they gone?  8 she has left;  9 he was the first;  10 you have been kind.

VOCABULARY: rose, **rosa** *f*; the worst, **il peggio** (pej-jo)

**35.** The DIRECT OBJECT PRONOUNS are:

| me | **mi** | us | **ci** |
|---|---|---|---|
| you (*fam*) | **ti** | you | **vi** |
| him, it | **lo** | them | **li** *m* |
| her, it | **la** | them | **le** *f* |
| you (*pol*) | **La** *m/f sing* | you (*pol*) | **Li** *m pl* |
| | | you (*pol*) | **Le** *f pl* |

They are placed immediately before the verb, except in a few cases which will be explained later:

| we believe you | **ti crediamo** |
|---|---|
| I invite you | **vi invito** |
| they serve him | **lo servono** |
| you invite us | **Lei c'invita** |

**Lo, la** and (less frequently) **mi, ti, vi** drop the vowel and take an apostrophe before a verb beginning with a vowel or h (Present Tense of **avere**); **ci** becomes **c'** only before e or i.

## EXERCISE III

1 we found a strange flower: do you know it?; 2 no, we have never seen it before; 3 we have studied these subjects; 4 I have forgotten them; 5 they have asked them; 6 where have you been?; 7 I looked for you everywhere; 8 I am sorry, sir, the manager cannot see you today, but he will see you tomorrow at 11 o'clock.

VOCABULARY: strange, **strano** or **raro** (strah-noh, rah-roh); to know, **conóscere** (co-nó-sheh-reh); before, **prima**; subject, **materia** *f* (mahteh-re'ah); to forget, **dimenticare** (de-men-te-car-eh); to ask, **domandare**; to look for someone, **cercare** (cher-car-eh) **uno**; everywhere, **dappertutto**; I am sorry, **mi dispiace** (dis-pe'-ah-cheh); manager, **direttore** *m* (de-reht-toh-reh); cannot, **non può**; to see, **vedere** or **ricévere** (re-chéh-ver-eh); today, **oggi** (oh-jjee); tomorrow, **domani** (dom-ah-nee).

## CONVERSATION

| | |
|---|---|
| Che cosa c'è questa[1] sera[2] alla TV[3]? | What is there on the TV this evening? |
| Sul primo canale[4] c'è uno spettácolo[5] di varietà[6], con la partecipazione[7] di Milva[8] e di altri cantanti[9]. Sul secondo canale c'è una commedia[10] di Eduardo[11] De Filippo[12]. | On the first channel there is a variety show with Milva and other singers. On the second channel there is a play by Eduardo De Filippo. |
| Davvero[13]? E' sempre[14] un piacere per me rivedere Eduardo, così umano e divertente[15]. | Really? I always enjoy seeing Eduardo: he is so human and entertaining. |
| Anche per me. Allora[16], non dimenticare: alle nove sul secondo canale! | So do I. Don't forget, then: at 9 o'clock on the second channel! |

PRONUNCIATION: 1 ques-tah; 2 seh-rah; 3 tv, tee-voo (televisione, teh-leh-vee-see-oh-neh); 4 can-ah-leh; 5 spet-táh-coh-loh; 6 vah-rih-ehtáh; 7 pahr-teh-chee-pah-tse'o-neh; 8 Meel-vah; 9 cahn-tahn-tee; 10 com-meh-dee-ah; 11 Eh-doo'ahr-doh; 12 Deh-fee-leep-oh; 13 davveh-roh; 14 sem-preh; 15 dee-verr-ten-teh; 16 ahl-loh-rah.

# LESSON SEVEN

**36.** The FUTURE TENSE is formed by adding the characteristic endings to the infinitive, after dropping the last *e*. In First Conjugation verbs **ar-** becomes **er-**, thus:

I shall speak
you will speak *etc.*

parler-ò (par-leh-ròh)
parler-ài (par-leh-rà'ee)
parler-à (par-leh-ràh)
parler-emo (par-leh-reh-moh)
parler-ete (par-leh-reh-teh)
parler-anno (par-leh-rah-nno)

| I shall believe *etc.* | | I shall finish *etc.* | |
|---|---|---|---|
| crederò | | | finirò |
| crederài | | | finirài |
| crederà | | | finirà |
| crederemo | | | finiremo |
| crederete | | | finirete |
| crederanno | | | finiranno |

**37.** The Future Tense of **essere** and **avere** does not follow the general pattern, although the endings are the same.

| I shall be *etc.* | | I shall have *etc.* | |
|---|---|---|---|
| sarò (sah-ròh) | | | avrò (ah-vròh) |
| sarài | | | avrài |
| sarà | | | avrà |
| saremo | | | avremo |
| sarete | | | avrete |
| saranno | | | avranno |

# EXERCISE I

1 will you live together?; 2 will they bring enough ice-cream?; 3 will you be ready at three o'clock, Teresa?; 4 certainly, I shall be the one to wait for you; 5 will you have much work?; 6 yes, but it will be interesting; 7 will you (*fam*) tell us about it?; 8 my wife will tell you everything; 9 we shall visit Roma first, then Bologna; 10 they will come back at dinner time.

VOCABULARY: enough, **abbastanza** (ab-bah-stan-tsah); ice-cream, **gelato** *m* (jeh-lah-toh); ready, **pronto** (pron-toh); **Teresa** (teh-reh-sah); work, **lavoro** *m* (lah-vor-oh); interesting, **interessante** (in-te-ress-ahn-teh); to tell, **raccontare, dire** (dee-reh); wife, **moglie** *f* (moh-l'yeh); everything, **tutto** (too-ttoh); to visit, **visitare** (ve-see-tar-eh); Roh-mah; Bol-oh-n'yah; then, **poi** (poee); to come back, **tornare** (torr-nar-eh); dinner, **cena** *f* (cheh-nah).

**38.** WHO? WHAT? WHICH? are translated **chi?**, **che** or **che cosa?** and **quale?**

| | |
|---|---|
| Who is first? | Chi è il primo? |
| What happened? | Che è successo? |
| What would you (*pol.*) like? | Che cosa desídera (or desíderano)? |
| Which papers does he buy? | Quali giornali compra? |

**39.** Another interrogative adjective and pronoun is **quanto** (quahn-to), which in various ways related to quantity:

| | |
|---|---|
| How much is this? | Quanto costa? |
| | Quanto fa? |
| How many chairs are there? | Quante sedie ci sono? |
| What a long time I have waited! | Quanto tempo ho aspettato! |

34

## EXERCISE II

1 how many people have you invited?; 2 tell me which clothes I must wear; 3 what are you looking for?; 4 who is playing with Miss Ross?; 5 which is my room?; 6 would whoever has taken the key to the laboratory please put it back in its place; 7 what have you done?; 8 Mr. Martelli would like to know how much he owes you.

VOCABULARY: people, **persone** *f, pl.* (perr-so-neh); clothes, **vestiti** or **vestito** *m* (ves-tee-toh); to wear, **méttere** or **portare**; to look for, **cercare** (cher-car-eh); to play, **giocare** (jo-car-eh); taken, **preso** (preh-soh); key, **chiave** *f* (ke'ah-veh); laboratory, **laboratório** *m*; to put back, **riméttere**; done, **fatto** (fah-ttoh); to know, **sapere** *and* **conóscere** (sah-pereh); to owe, **dovere** (doh-veh-reh).

## CONVERSAZIONE

How do you say in Italian: 21, 31, 41, etc.?

Come[1] si dice[2] in italiano: 21, 31, 41? Si dice: ventuno[3], trentuno, quarantuno eccétera[4].

In that case, venti, trenta drop the last letter before uno.

Allora vuol dire che venti, trenta pérdono l'última[5] léttera davanti[6] a uno.

And before otto, since 28 is read ventotto.

Anche davanti a 8, poiché[7] 28 si legge[8] ventotto.

I see. It's quite easy: ventuno, ventotto, but: ventidue, ventinove.

Capisco[9]. E' facile[10]: si dice ventuno, ventotto, ma: ventidue, ventinove.

The same applies, of course, to trentuno, trentadue; quarantuno, quarantadue, and so on and so forth.

La stessa[11] cosa, naturalmente[12], vale[13] per 31, 32; 41, 42, e così via[14].

PRONUNCIATION: 1 coh-meh; 2 dee-cheh; 3 ven-too-noh; 4 eh-ché-teh-rah; 5 oól-te-moh; 6 dah-van-tee; 7 po'e-káy; 8 leh-jeh; 9 cap-ee-scoh; 10 fáh-chee-leh; 11 steh-ssoh; 12 nah-too-ral-men-teh; 13 vah-leh; 14 vee-ah.

35

**40.** A few nouns and adjectives must be noted for their plural: those ending in **-co, -go**.

| | | | |
|---|---|---|---|
| friend | **amico** | **amici** | (ah-mee-chee) |
| authentic | **auténtico** | **auténtici** | (a'oo-tén-tee-chee) |
| asparagus | **asparago** | **asparagi** | (ahss-pah-rah-jee) |

An **h** is added when the letter before **-co, -go** is different from *i*, and in all the feminine counterparts, which of course end in **-ca, -ga**:

| | | | |
|---|---|---|---|
| white | **bianco** | **bianchi** | (be'an-kee) |
| | **bianca** | **bianche** | (be'an-keh) |
| sorcerer | **mago** | **maghi** | (mah-ghe) |
| sorceress | **maga** | **maghe** | (mah-gay) |

However, these rules have many exceptions, which can only be learnt by practice.

| | | | |
|---|---|---|---|
| ancient | **antico** | **antichi** | (ahn-tee-kee) |
| psychologist | **psicólogo** | **psicólogi** | (pse-có-lo-gee) |

## EXERCISE III

1 (a) few days;   2 the banks;   3 the ancient Greeks;   4 they are loaded with parcels;   5 German archaeologists;   6 in the shops.

VOCABULARY: few, **poco**; bank, **banca** *f* (bahn-kah); Greek, **greco** (greh-koh); loaded, **cárico** (káh-re-koh); parcel, **pacco** *m* (pah-koh); German, **tedesco** (teh-des-koh); archaeologist, **archeólogo** *m* (ahr-keh-óh-lo-go); shop, **bottega** *f* (bot-teh-ga).

## CONVERSATION

| | |
|---|---|
| Come ti chiami[1]? | What is your name? |
| Michele.[2] | Michele. |
| Io mi chiamo Alan e ho dieci anni. Tu quanti anni hai? | My name is Alan and I am ten years old. How old are you? |
| Nove. | Nine. |

36

| | |
|---|---|
| Ah, mi pareva³! Allora non saremo⁴ nella stessa⁵ classe.⁶ Io sono in quinta. | I thought so. That means we shall not be in the same year. I am in the fifth. |
| E io sono in quarta. | And I'm in the fourth. |
| Peccato! Ci vedremo⁷ durante⁸ la ricreazione.⁹ | Pity! We shall see one another at break. |

PRONUNCIATION: 1 ke'ah-me; 2 mee-keh-leh; 3 pah-reh-vah; 4 sah-reh-moh; 5 stess-ah; 6 class-eh; 7 veh-dre-moh; 8 doo-ran-teh; 9 ree-creh-ah-ts'e-o-neh.

# LESSON EIGHT

## 41. THE IMPERATIVE MOOD

| parla, parlate | credi, credete | servi, servite |
|---|---|---|
| *speak* | *believe* | *serve* |

**Parla** is the only Imperative which differs from the Present Indicative second person. In Italian, this mood of the verb belongs to the familiar form; the polite form, as we shall see later on, uses the Subjunctive.

## EXERCISE I

1 listen!;  2 wait;  3 finish up the bottle;  4 turn off the light;  5 turn it on;  6 go to sleep.

VOCABULARY: to finish up, **finire**; to turn off, **spégnere** (spéh-n'yeh-reh); to turn on, **accéndere** (ah-chén-deh-reh); to go to sleep, **dormire** (dor-mee-reh).

## 42. PRESENT SUBJUNCTIVE OF ESSERE, AVERE

| che io sia | che io abbia |
|---|---|
| sia | abbia |
| sia | abbia |
| siamo | abbiamo |
| siate | abbiate |
| síano | ábbiano |

| | |
|---|---|
| I believe it is preferable. | **Credo che sia preferíbile.** |
| Let's hope he has that book. | **Speriamo che abbia quel libro.** |
| Have mercy on me! | **Abbiate pietà di me!** |

As can be seen from the third example, **siate** and **abbiate** are also used as plural imperatives, along with **sii** and **abbi** in the singular.

More instruction on the Subjunctive is in Lesson Thirteen.

**43.** DON'T BE, DON'T HAVE and (generally) DON'T + VERB are translated in this manner:

| | |
|---|---|
| Don't be late | **Non essere in ritardo** (tu) |
| | **Non siate in ritardo** (voi) |
| Don't sing | **Non cantare** (tu) |
| | **Non cantate** (voi) |

## EXERCISE II

(Both singular and plural must be given.) 1 run; 2 don't be afraid; 3 don't open the door; 4 go slowly; 5 don't be nosy; 6 be on time; 7 have faith; 8 don't be in a hurry.

VOCABULARY: to run, **córrere** (kóhr-reh-reh); to be afraid, **aver paúra** (pa'oó-rah); to open, **aprire** (ah-pree-reh); nosy, **curioso** (koo-ree-o-zo); to be on time, **essere puntuale** (poon-too-ah-leh); faith, **fede** *f* (feh-deh); to be in a hurry, **aver fretta** freh-ttah).

**44.** The INDIRECT OBJECT PRONOUNS are:

| | |
|---|---|
| to me | **mi** |
| to you | **ti** |
| to him, it | **ģli** |
| to her, it | **le** |
| to us | **ci** |
| to you | **vi** |
| to them | **loro** |

Like the other pronouns in §35, these pronouns go immediately before the verb. In spoken Italian **gli** is commonly used instead of **loro**, the only one that follows the verb.

| | |
|---|---|
| Will you write to me? | **Mi scriverai?** |
| Anna forwards his mail to him. | **Anna gli gira la posta.** |
| The teacher gives them the books | **Il maestro dà loro i libri.** |

## EXERCISE III

1 I shall reply to you (*fam*) at once;    2 she is repeating to you his words;    3 they are taking her some sweets;    4 you (voi) will speak to him, then?;    5 the control tower gives them the position;    6 this book is dedicated to me.

VOCABULARY: to reply, **rispóndere** (rees-pón-dereh); to repeat, **ripétere** (re-péh-teh-reh); word, **parola** *f* (pah-ro-lah); sweet, **caramella** *f* (car-ah-mel-lah); control tower, **torre** (*f*) **di controllo** *m* (toh-rreh con-troll-oh); to give, **dare** (dah-reh); position, **posizione** *f* (po-ze-tse'o-neh); to dedicate, **dedicare** (deh-dee-kah-reh).

## CONVERSATION

| | |
|---|---|
| What are you looking for? | Che cosa cerchi[1]? |
| My cap. It has disappeared. | Il mio berretto[2]. E' sparito[3]. |
| Where did you leave it yesterday evening? | Dove l'hai lasciato[4] ieri[5] sera? |
| In the hall. | Nell'entrata[6]. |
| Are you sure it is not still there? | Sei sicuro[7] che non sia ancora[8] lì[9]? |
| It is not there. I have already looked. | Non c'è. Ho già[10] guardato[11]. |
| Perhaps your brother took it, by mistake? | Che l'abbia preso tuo fratello, per sbaglio? |
| Whoever took it, what am I going to do? | Chiunque[12] l'abbia preso, io come farò[13]? |

PRONUNCIATION: 1 chair-ke; 2 beh-rret-toh; 3 spah-ree-toh; 4 lash-ah-toh; 5 e'eh-ree; 6 en-trah-tah; 7 see-coo-roh; 8 ahn-cor-ah; 9 lee; 10 je'ah; 11 goo'ar-dah-toh; 12 kee-oon-queh; 13 fah-ròh.

# LESSON NINE

**45.** MORE, LESS . . . THAN are translated **più, meno . . . di** (or **che**).

| | |
|---|---|
| There is more mud than water. | C'è più fango che acqua. |
| They sell less wine than us. | Vendono meno vino di noi. |
| You are more active than Sandra. | Sei più attiva di Sandra. |
| They have less books than magazines. | Hanno meno libri che riviste. |

**46.** Adjectives ending with **-er, -est** are translated **più . . ., il più . . .,** thus

| | |
|---|---|
| taller, tallest | **più alto, il più alto** |
| kinder, kindest | **più gentile, il più gentile** |

## EXERCISE I

1 the second volume is more important than the first; 2 there are less inhabitants in the villages; 3 the French restaurant is nicer; 4 it is also more expensive; 5 who has the highest number?; 6 the lowest card wins.

VOCABULARY: volume, **volume** *m* (vol-oo-meh); important, **importante** (im-porr-tan-teh); inhabitant, **abitante** *m* (ah-be-tahn-teh); village, **paése** *m* (pah-éh-seh); French, **francese** (fran-cheh-seh); restaurant, **ristorante** *m* (ris-to-ran-teh); nice, **simpático** (sim-pah-te-coh); expensive (dear) **caro** (cah-roh); number, **número** *m* (noo-meh-roh); high, tall, **alto** (ahl-toh); low, **basso** (bah-sso); to win, **víncere** (vín-cheh-reh)

**47.** WHO, WHOSE, WHOM; WHICH, THAT are translated **che, cui; che.**

| | |
|---|---|
| The girl who is going to play . . . | La ragazza che suonerà . . . |
| Puccini, whose operas you know . . . | Puccini, le cui ópere conoscete (or: di cui conoscete le ópere . . .) |
| James, whom everyone admires . . . | Giácomo, che tutti ammirano . . . |
| The method which has been explained . . . | Il metodo che è stato stiegato . . . |
| The parcel that he opened . . . | Il pacco che ha aperto . . . |

40

**48.** WHOM, WHICH used with prepositions become **cui:**

| | |
|---|---|
| The lady from whom we receive so many letters . . . | **La signora da cui riceviamo tante lettere . . .** |
| The magazine to which you have subscribed . . . | **La rivista a cui siete abbonati . . .** |
| The room I told you about . . . | **La stanza di cui ti ho parlato . . .** |

Notice the last example: in Italian the relative pronoun must be expressed and it follows immediately the noun it refers to.

**49.** Che and **cui** are doubled by another series of relative pronouns, less used because they are more cumbersome:

> **il quale,  la quale**
> **i quali,   le quali**

You need not use them at all: but it is equally correct to say

| | |
|---|---|
| The car I travel in is a Fiat. | **La macchina con cui viaggio è una Fiat.** |
| | **La macchina con la quale viaggio è una Fiat.** |

## EXERCISE II

1 here is Peter, whose parents you have already met;  2 the young man that you accompanied to the station is very nice; 3 the gentleman who is going to give us a talk will be here soon; 4 they had a daughter, whom they loved dearly;  5 I can see children playing and parents drinking beer;  6 the people Sara works with are German.

VOCABULARY: Peter, **Pietro** (pe'éh-troh); met, **conosciuto** (con-oh-shoo-toh); parents, **genitori** (jeh-nee-tor-ee); young man, **giovane** *m*; to give a talk, **fare una conferenza** (con-feh-ren-tsah, *f*); to love, **amare** (ah-ma-reh); dearly, **teneramente** (ten-eh-rah-men-teh); can, **posso** (*not translated here, though*); to see, **vedere** (veh-deh-reh); drinking, **che bévono** (keh béh-voh-noh); beer, **birra** *f* (beer-rah); people, **le persone** ; German, **tedesco.**

41

**50.** There are only four irregular verbs in the First Conjugation, but they are used a lot, as they appear in many idioms. They are:

> **dare** (dah-reh), to give
> **andare** (ahn-dah-reh), to go
> **fare** (fah-reh), to make, to do
> **stare** (stah-reh), to stay, to be.

**PRESENT TENSE**

| I go, *etc.* | I give, *etc.* | I do, *etc.* | I stay, *etc.* |
|---|---|---|---|
| vado | do | faccio | sto |
| vai | dai | fai | stai |
| va | dà | fa | sta |
| andiamo | diamo | facciamo | stiamo |
| andate | date | fate | state |
| vanno | danno | fanno | stanno |

**PAST PARTICIPLE**

andato, gone      dato, given      fatto, done/made
stato, been

Remember that *I have been, I have gone* become **sono stato, sono andato** (§34).

**IMPERATIVE**

| go | give | do | stay |
|---|---|---|---|
| va' | da' | fa' | sta' |
| andate | date | fate | state |

Notice that the singular forms **va', da'**, etc., are more frequently used than the ordinary forms **vai, dai, fai, stai**.

## EXERCISE III

1 are you going by car or by plane?;  2 the farmer goes to market;  3 my mother does it like that;  4 cigarettes are bad for you;  5 will you give me that plate, please?;  6 how much

will they give you for the work you have done?;  7 you haven't been careful;  8 we are always careful;  9 do as I told you; 10 go, and come back soon;  11 give to Caesar that which is Caesar's;  12 have you watered the plants?

VOCABULARY: car, **mácchina** *f*, **áuto** *f* (máhk-kee-nah, áh'oo-toh); farmer, **contadino** *m* (con-tah-dee-noh); market, **mercato** *m* (mehr-cah-toh); cigarette, **sigaretta** *f* (see-gah-reh-tta); (to be) bad for, **fare male** (*literally*: to do badly); plate, **piatto** *m* (pe'ah-ttoh); work, **lavoro** *m* (lah-voroh); careful, **attento** (aht-ten-toh); soon, **presto** (preh-stoh); Caesar, **Césare** (Chéh-zah-reh); to water, **dare l'acqua** *f* (ah-kwah); plant, **pianta** *f* (piahn-ta).

## CONVERSATION

Ciao, Giácomo! Sei già di ritorno[1]?

Hallo, James, are you back already?

Sono tornato ieri. Sono stato fuori[2] quattro giorni[3].

I got back yesterday. I've been away four days.

Com'è andata?

How did it go?

Non c'è male[4]. Ho sbrigato[5] i miei affari[6], poi ho fatto una vísita[7] a dei parenti[8] e l'ultimo giorno sono andato a spasso[9] e a fare spese[10].

Not too badly. I did what I had to, then I visited some relations and on the last day I walked around and did some shopping.

Hai fatto bene. Dove sei stato di bello?

Good for you. Did you go anywhere interesting?

Ho visitato la Piazza[11] Maggiore[12] e la Cattedrale[13], ho pranzato[14] alla trattoria[15] dei Tre Mori[16] e ho fatto tutto[17] il Corso[18], su[19] e giù[20], prima di entrare[21] da Valli[22], quel famoso[23] negozio di stampe[24] e riproduzioni[25] artístiche[26].

I went to The Square and the Cathedral, I had lunch at the Three Moors Restaurant and I walked up and down the main street before going into Valli's, that famous shop where they sell prints and artistic reproductions.

PRONUNCIATION: 1 ree-torr-noh; 2 foo'ó-ree; 3 je'or-nee; 4 mah-leh; 5 sbree-gah-toh; 6 ahf-fah-ree; 7 veé-se-tah; 8 pah-ren-tee; 9 spah-ssoh; 10 speh-seh; 11 pe'ah-tsa; 12 mahd-jor-eh; 13 cat-teh-drah-leh; 14 pran-tsato; 15 trat-toh-reéa; 16 moh-ree; 17 too-tto (*all*, *whole*); 18 corr-so; 19 soo; 20 joo; 21 ent-rah-reh; 22 vah-llee; 23 fah-mo-zo; 24 stahm-peh; 25 ree-pro-doot-se'oh-nee; 26 arr-tís-tee-keh.

From now on, pronunciation will be given only in those cases where the basic rules stated in the Introduction are disregarded.

## LESSON TEN

**51.** Linking up with the pronouns studied in §35, there are two more to be learnt: **ne** and **ci (vi)**.

Referring to a noun or an action previously mentioned, **ne** means *some, any, about that* or *about it.*

| | |
|---|---|
| Have you any blankets? Yes, we have some. | **Avete delle coperte? Sì, ne abbiamo.** |
| Has John told you about his adventure? He was just telling me about it. | **Giovanni ti ha raccontato la sua avventura? Ne parlava proprio ora.** |

Used as an adverb, **ne** means 'from there'.

| | |
|---|---|
| Are they coming from Beirut? They left there four hours ago. | **Vengono da Beirut? Ne sono partiti quattro ore fa.** |

**Ci** is used very frequently as an adverb, meaning *to there*, and sometimes referring to something already mentioned, meaning *to, about that.*

| | |
|---|---|
| Aren't you thinking about your career? Yes, I am thinking about it. | **Non pensi alla tua carriera? Sì, ci penso.** |
| Are you really going to Edinburgh? Yes, I am going there on the 15th. | **Davvero vai a Edimburgo? Sì, ci vado il 15.** |
| Aren't you working any more? No, I'm not going there any more. | **Non vai più a lavorare? No, non ci vado più.** |

### EXERCISE I

1 Peter has had three presents, perhaps tomorrow he will have another one;   2 John's boat is fantastic, we too are going to have one like it;   3 they have been to Genoa once, and they are going again this year;   4 an earthquake, whoever would have thought of it?

VOCABULARY: perhaps, **forse**; another one, **un altro**; boat, **barca** *f*; fantastic, **stupendo**; Genoa, **Genova** (jéh-no-vah); once, **una volta**; again, **di nuovo**; earthquake, **terremoto** *m*.

44

**52.** DEMONSTRATIVE ADJECTIVES AND PRONOUNS

*This, this one, these* are translated **questo/a, questi/e**; *that, that one, those* are translated **quello/a, ciò, quelli/e**.

| | |
|---|---|
| We are going to take these books and leave those. | Prendiamo questi libri e lasciamo quelli. |
| Those cities were much poorer than this one. | Quelle città érano molto più povere di questa. |
| This one is all right, that one isn't. | Questo va bene, quello no. |
| Apart from that . . . | A parte ciò . . . |
| We shall talk about that later. | Parleremo dopo di ciò. |

**53.** A special mention should be made of alternative forms of **quello** and **quelli** when used as adjectives. The pattern is the same as that followed by the definite article (see §7 and §8):

| | |
|---|---|
| that tree, those trees | quell'albero, quegli alberi |
| that flower, those flowers | quel fiore, quei fiori |
| that mistake, those mistakes | quello sbaglio, quegli sbagli |

**54.** Quello (quel) and ciò can be followed by **che**; the English equivalent of **ciò che** is *what*.

| | |
|---|---|
| I'll give you what I have. | Vi do quello che ho. |
| What matters is what they do, not what they say. | Ciò che importa è quello che fanno, non quello che dícono |

## EXERCISE II

1 this time we have not earned much;  2 take what you need;  3 I don't understand that woman;  4 if you want to visit the gardens, ask this man;  5 look at the deer by the river!;  6 those animals have become rare;  7 Peter, that idiot, has killed one;  8 he'll have to pay for this.

VOCABULARY: to earn, **guadagnare**; to take, **préndere**; you need, **vi serve**; to want, **volere**; to ask, **chiédere**; a man, **uomo** *m*; woman, **donna** *f*; deer, **daino/i**; river, **fiume** *m*; animal, **animale** *m*; to become, **diventare** (*aux.* **essere**); rare, **raro**; idiot, **sciocco, idiota**; killed, **ucciso**; to pay, **pagare**.

**55.** THE CONDITIONAL TENSE. Like the Future, this tense is formed from the Infinitive stem.

| -are | -ere | -ire |
|---|---|---|
| *I should speak* | *I should believe* | *I should finish* |
| parler-ei | creder-ei | finir-ei |
| parler-esti | creder-esti | finir-esti |
| parler-ebbe | creder-ebbe | finir-ebbe |
| parler-emmo | creder-emmo | finir-emmo |
| parler-este | creder-este | finir-este |
| parler-ébbero | creder ébbero | finir-ébbero |

Note the third person endings, **-ebbe, -ébbero.** This tense expresses the possibility or the wish that something may occur at the time of speaking or in the future.

| We would take the 8 o'clock train. | **Prenderemmo il treno delle 8.** |
|---|---|
| Would you live on the top floor? | **Abiteresti all'ultimo piano?** |
| In his position I would look for another job. | **Al suo posto, io cercherei un altro lavoro.** |

**56.** The Conditional Tense of **avere, essere.**

| *I should have* | *I should be* |
|---|---|
| avrei | sarei |
| avresti | saresti |
| avrebbe | sarebbe |
| avremmo | saremmo |
| avreste | sareste |
| avrébbero | sarébbero |

## EXERCISE III

1 would you lend me the Russian dictionary?;  2 what would you say if we went out for an hour?;  3 Mario would be glad to see you;  4 I should think so;  5 the couple on the fourth floor should have a room to let;  6 would you like to see it?

VOCABULARY: to lend, **imprestare**; Russian, **russo**; dictionary, **dizionario**; to go out, **uscire**; glad, **contento**; to see you, **di vedervi**; couple, **coppia** *f*; to let, **affittare**; room, **stanza** *f*; to like: *in questions like this one, the conditional becomes the present tense of* **volere.**

46

# CONVERSATION

Vorrei imparare i giorni della settimana. C'è una filastrocca apposta, per i bambini?

I should like to learn the days of the week. Is there a children's nursery rhyme for that?

Ce ne sarebbe una, intitolata 'Verrà quel dì di lune', ma non è adatta perché è in dialetto . . .

There is one, called 'That Moonday will come', but it is not suitable, because it is in dialect.

Peccato! Tutte le filastrocche sono in dialetto?

A pity! Are all nursery rhymes in dialect?

Sì, in gran parte. Ad ogni modo, ecco i giorni della settimana: lunedì, martedì, mercoledì, giovedì, venerdì, sábato, doménica.

Yes, many of them are. Anyway, here are the days of the week: Monday, Tuesday, Wednesday, Thursday, Friday, Saturday, Sunday.

Gli ultimi due sono diversi dai primi cinque, cioè non sono formati con 'dì'.

The last two are different from the first five; that is, they are not formed with 'dì'.

E' vero. E attenzione all'articolo; dirai: 'Lavoro dal lunedì al venerdì, il sábato e la doménica mi riposo'. La doménica, dunque, è un nome femminile.

That's right. And be careful with the article. You must say 'I work from (the) Monday to (the) Friday, and rest (the) Saturday and (the) Sunday. La doménica, then, is a feminine noun.

---

Remember: the grave (`) accent on **Lunedì** etc. is obligatory in type; the acute (´) we show on **sábato** and **doménica** purely as a guide to correct pronunciation. In later extracts these words will be printed without an acute accent.

**57.** The IMPERFECT TENSE is used frequently in Italian. In many cases, the English equivalent is the continuous form, e.g. *I was speaking, I was finishing*, etc.:

| parl-avo | cred-evo | fin-ivo |
|----------|----------|---------|
| parl-avi | cred-evi | fin-ivi |
| parl-ava | cred-eva | fin-iva |
| parl-avamo | cred-evamo | fin-ivamo |
| parl-avate | cred-evate | fin-ivate |
| parl-ávano | cred-évano | fin-ívano |

**58.** The Imperfect Tense of **avere, essere.**

| avevo | ero |
|-------|-----|
| avevi | eri |
| aveva | era |
| avevamo | eravamo |
| avevate | eravate |
| avévano | érano |

| | |
|---|---|
| It was evening; Teresa was reading. | **Era sera; Teresa leggeva.** |
| They lived in a small flat in town. | **Stavano in città in un píccolo appartamento.** |
| We arrived when James was speaking. | **Siamo arrivati quando parlava Giacomo.** |
| When you were small we went to the seaside every summer. | **Quando eravate piccoli, ogni estate andavamo al mare.** |

As has been shown, the Imperfect is used: 1) for descriptions in the past; 2) for background narrations; 3) to express what was going on when something else happened; 4) to express an action repeated a number of times in the past.

## EXERCISE I

1 were those letters all right? Yes, thank you, I have already sent them;   2 the stranger's bad mood lasted two or three days, then it passed and he talked once again with everyone;   3 while the sister closed the suitcase, Albert telephoned for a taxi;   4 on Monday evenings they played cards and on Fridays they played billiards in a bar.

VOCABULARY: letter, **léttera** *f*; sent, **spedito**; stranger, **straniero/a**; bad mood, **malumore** *m*; to last, **durare**; to talk, **parlare**; once again, **di nuovo**; to close, **chiúdere**; suitcase, **valigia** *f*; taxi, **tassi** *m*; cards, **carte** *f*; billiards, **bigliardo** *m*.

**59.**   Rules on the positions of adjectives are flexible in Italian. Most adjectives follow the noun they qualify, but this can be reversed in order to put emphasis on the adjective.

| | |
|---|---|
| a difficult job | **un lavoro difficile** |
| a *difficult* job | **un difficile lavoro** |
| a life of hard work | **una vita laboriosa** |
| a life of pleasure | **la dolce vita** |

Common and short adjectives, such as **dolce**, **buono**, etc., tend to go before the noun; on the other hand, adjectives stating colour, shape and nationality, follow it:

| | |
|---|---|
| the square table | **il tavolo quadrato** |
| the green boxes | **le scátole verdi** |

Irregular adjectives are dealt with in the Appendix.

## EXERCISE II

1 this is a good material and costs more;   2 that intelligent, courageous man will find a solution;   3 your old aunt has been up to her tricks again;   4 there is some very bad news today; 5 the barometer says 'changeable';   6 this calm sea and blue sky will last for about three days;   7 the journey was horrible, but fortunately it was short;   8 short reckoning makes long friends (patti chiari amicizia lunga).

VOCABULARY: material, **stoffa** *f*; to cost, **costare**; courageous **coraggioso**; solution, **soluzione** *f*; old, **vecchio**; to be up to one's tricks, **combinarla bella**; bad, **brutto** *or* **cattivo**; news **notizia/e** *f*; barometer, **barómetro** *m*; changeable, **variábile**; calm, **calmo**; blue, **azzurro**; sky, **cielo** *m*; about, **circa**; horrible, **orríbile**; short, **corto**.

**60.** *I like, Albert likes*, etc. are translated **mi piace, ad Alberto piace**, etc., which literally mean: *it pleases me, Albert*, etc.

| | |
|---|---|
| Do you like my dress? | **Ti piace il mio vestito?** |
| We like to read the paper on Sundays. | **La domenica ci piace leggere il giornale.** |
| I like oranges. | **Mi piácciono le arance.** |
| Teresa likes adventure books. | **A Teresa piácciono i libri di avventure.** |

**Piácciono** is the plural of **piace** and is used when more than one 'thing' is liked.

For the past (*did you like?*) there is **ti è piaciuto?**; for the future (*will you like?*), **ti piacerà?**; for the conditional, **ti piacerebbe?** (*would you like?*).

## EXERCISE III

1 the count did not like the architect's design; 2 cats don't like water; 3 he would like to go on a journey. What about you? 4 this is your (*polite form*) room. I hope you will like it; 5 the butler says that your friend likes antique furniture.

VOCABULARY: count, **conte** *m*; architect, **architetto** *m*; design, **disegno** *m*; cat, **gatto** *m*; butler, **maggiordomo** *m*; furniture, **móbili** *m*.

**61.** THE DATE

As in English, dates are normally written in figures; for the present century they are also shortened (**nel '30, nel '75**). Notice the way in which a whole century is indicated.

| | |
|---|---|
| What is the date? | **Che giorno è?** |
| April 20th. | **Il 20 aprile.** |
| In 1930. | **Nel millenovecentotrenta, nel Trenta. (nel '30)** |
| The XIXth century. | **L'Ottocento (il 19° sécolo, il XIX sécolo).** |

50

# CONVERSATION

| | |
|---|---|
| Dicono che c'era molta gente a Viareggio per Ferragosto. | They say there were lots of people at Viareggio on the (August) Bank holiday. |
| Moltissima: il tempo era óttimo, il lungomare era gremito di automóbili, sulla spiaggia i bagnanti stavano gómito a gómito. | Yes, lots: the weather was excellent, the promenade was packed with cars and on the beach the bathers sat elbow to elbow. |
| Hm! Tutte cose che a te non piacciono, mi pare. | Hm! All the things that you dislike, I believe. |
| Infatti: non sono neanche entrato in città, ho preso una strada che saliva verso la montagna e sono sceso in una località pittoresca. Poiché non c'era nessuno, ho passato una bella giornata. | Exactly; so I didn't even go into town, instead I drove up a road which climbed towards the mountains and I stopped at a picturesque spot. As nobody was around, I had a lovely day. |

**62.** The following are among the most important irregular verbs belonging to the second Conjugation:

| *I want* | *I can* | *I must* | *I know* |
|---|---|---|---|
| voglio | posso | devo (debbo) | so |
| vuoi | puoi | devi | sai |
| vuole | può | deve | sa |
| vogliamo | possiamo | dobbiamo | sappiamo |
| volete | potete | dovete | sapete |
| vógliono | póssono | dévono (débbono) | sanno |

Infinitive: volere; potere; dovere; sapere. Past participle: voluto; potuto; dovuto; saputo.

51

These verbs have all got several meanings, apart from the basic one: **voglio**, *I will, I wish*; **posso**, *I may*; **devo**, *I have to*; **sapere**, on the other hand, only means *to know how*, or a fact, not 'to be acquainted' with a person or place.

## CONVERSATION

Adesso potete fare quello che volete: siete líberi fino alle quattro e un quarto. Il nostro autista vuole partire alle 4,30 in punto, perciò tutti devono tornare al torpedone in tempo.

Now you can do what you wish: you are free until 4.15. Our driver wants to leave punctually at 4.30 so everybody must be back at the coach on time.

Signorina, possiamo fare il giro del laghetto?

Miss, may we go round the pond?

E noi possiamo tornare al chiosco degli oggetti-ricordo?

And can we go back to the kiosk where they sell souvenirs?

Noi siamo stanchi e restiamo qui sulle panchine.

We are tired; we are staying here on the benches.

Andate, e ricordate quello che vi ho detto. Finalmente la signorina Bianchi e io potremo andare a prendere un caffè.

Off you go and remember what I have said. At last Miss Bianchi and I can go and have a cup of coffee.

## EXERCISE IV

Transform the sentences in the first paragraph of the above Conversation by using all possible subjects. Example: Adesso posso fare quello che voglio . . .

# LESSON TWELVE

## 63. PRONOUN COMBINATIONS

You pass me the cup.    You pass it to me

become in Italian:

**Mi passi la tazza.**    **Me la passi.**

Similarly, in the other persons it runs

| | |
|---|---|
| We pass it to you | **Noi te/ve la passiamo** |
| The nurse gives it to us | **L'infermiera ce la dà** |
| The nurse gives it to him | **L'infermiera gliela dà** |
| The child gives it back to them | **Il bambino la rende loro** |

The above examples show the differences between English and Italian on this important point. You have realised that **mi, ti, ci, vi** become **me, te, ce, ve** when followed by **la, lo, le, li** (and **ne**). In the third person, **glielo** is used for both *it to him* and *it to her*; the same applies to the other possible combinations (**gliela, glieli, gliele**).

**Loro** follows both the direct pronoun and the verb. It is not used much, as the forms **glielo**, etc. tend to be extended to the plural.

## EXERCISE I

1 your book does not interest me; I am sorry, I shall give it back to you;   2 the landlady has some good wine; if you ask her she will give you some;   3 I told you that it would be good weather again today;   4 since the facts have been verified, I will tell them.

VOCABULARY: to interest, **interessare**; to be sorry, **dispiacere a uno**; landlady, **padrona** *f*, **di casa**; to ask, **chiédere**; fact, **fatto** *m*; to verify, **accertare**.

## 64. THE GERUND

| | | |
|---|---|---|
| *speaking* | *believing* | *finishing* |
| parl-ando | cred-endo | fin-endo |
| *being* | *having* | |
| ess-endo | av-endo | |

The gerund is used on its own, without a preposition, whereas the infinitive can be used with prepositions. There are several ways to translate the English gerund in Italian; notice in particular:

| | |
|---|---|
| by doing | **facendo, con il fare** |
| before writing | **prima di scrivere** |
| while finishing | **mentre (io) finivo** |
| on arriving | **arrivando, all'arrivo** |
| on leaving | **partendo, alla partenza** |

## 65. Essendo, avendo, are used on their own and as auxiliaries:

| | |
|---|---|
| having read, had | **avendo letto, avuto** |
| having gone, been | **essendo andato, stato** |

## EXERCISE II

1 coming to the economy of this area, we note that...; 2 you will get the best results using this product; 3 my brother-in-law will have a bargain if he buys that house; 4 having received the necessary information we can write the report on the accident; 5 since it has little coal or iron of its own, Italy has to import them.

VOCABULARY: to come, **venire**; economy, **economia** *f*; to note, osservare; to get, **ottenere (otterrò)**; the best, **óttimo**; result, **risultato** *m*; product, **prodotto** *m*; brother-in-law, **cognato** *m*; bargain, **affare** *m*; report, **rapporto** *m*; accident, **incidente** *m*; to have little, **essere povero di (aver poco** ...**)**; coal, **carbone** *m*; iron, **ferro** *m*; to import, **importare**; area, **regione** *f*.

## 66. Stare + *gerund* form the continuous tenses: Present, Imperfect, Future (to express what is likely to be happening).

| | |
|---|---|
| What is he doing? | **Che cosa sta facendo?** |
| He's washing the car. | **Sta lavando la macchina.** |
| Were you watching television? | **Stavate guardando la televisione?** |
| Emma must be going to bed. | **Emma starà andando a letto.** |

In Italian the continuous tenses express definite actions which are taking place over a certain time. On the other hand, *he is sleeping, reading*, etc., are normally rendered by **dorme, legge**, as already seen.

## EXERCISE III

1 Mr. Rondi is phoning;   2 the children are studying, they will come later;   3 the boat is coming;   4 we were talking about the trip.

VOCABULARY: to phone, **telefonare**; later, **più tardi**; boat, **battello** *m* or **barca** *f*; trip, **gita** *f*.

**67.** The Gerund, the Infinitive and the Imperative compound with direct and indirect object pronouns (see §62); if both of these are used, they join together and with the verbal word.

| | |
|---|---|
| It is your duty to wait for him. | **E' vostro dovere aspettarlo.** |
| Wait for him until 10 o'clock. | **Aspettátelo fino alle 10.** |
| Here's Daddy's present; may I give it to him straight away? | **Ecco il regalo per il babbo; posso dárglielo subito ?** |

Only **loro** is not linked:

| | |
|---|---|
| Telling them such a lie! | **Raccontare loro una menzogna símile!** |
| By writing to them that you will be coming on Sunday, you are obliging them to stay in. | **Scrivendo loro che arriverai domenica, li obblighi a stare in casa.** |

It must be noted that in a verb+pronoun combination the stress remains in the same position; that is, on the verb. The result is rather unexpected, as in the above example

$$\text{aspettate} + \text{lo} = \text{aspettátelo}$$

**68.** With the following Imperatives, the initial m, t, l, c, n of the attached pronoun is doubled:

va', vacci, go there          da', dallo, give it
fa', fanne, make some      sta', stammi vicino, stay close to me

55

**69.** Sometimes the English Gerund is translated by an Infinitive or a relative clause, as follows:

| | |
|---|---|
| I can see children playing. | **Vedo bambini che giocano.** |
| They could hear Linda singing. | **Sentivano cantare Linda,** *or* |
| | **Sentivano Linda che cantava.** |

## EXERCISE IV

1 Renato has got the ball. Get it from him;   2 give them back to me. Please, give them to me;   3 let's go away;   4 go away; 5 you have so many magazines, let us have some;   6 I was talking to him about it;   7 answering to them;   8 Teresa wrote asking to send her a photo;   9 let's send her one;   10 they could hear the masters having a terrible row.

VOCABULARY: ball, **palla** *f*; masters, **padroni** *m*; to have a row, **litigare**.

## CONVERSATION

| | |
|---|---|
| Come vanno le corde e i picchetti della tenda? | What are the guy-ropes (cords) and the tent pegs like? |
| E' quello che sto guardando; mi pare che siano a posto. | That's what I am looking at; I think they are all right. |
| Stai preparando qualcosa da mangiare? | Are you preparing anything to eat? |
| Sì, è quasi pronto. Hai notato che i pini fanno ombra proprio davanti alla nostra tenda? | Yes, it is nearly ready. Have you noticed that the pine trees throw shadows right in front of our tent? |
| Senza i pini farebbe un caldo insopportabile in questo campeggio. Hai già parlato con i nostri vicini? | Without the pine trees it would be unbearably hot in this camping site. Have you talked to our neighbours yet? |
| No, sono andati alla spiaggia prima di noi e non li ho più visti. Ma éccoli che tornano proprio adesso. | No, they went to the beach before us and I have not seen them since. There they are. They are coming back now. |

56

# LESSON THIRTEEN

## 70. THE SUBJUNCTIVE

### PRESENT TENSE

that I speak, believe, finish, *etc.*

| che io | parli | creda | finisca |
|--------|---------|----------|-----------|
| *etc.* | parli | creda | finisca |
| | parli | creda | finisca |
| | parliamo | crediamo | finiamo |
| | parliate | crediate | finiate |
| | párlino | crédano | finíscano |

that I am, have, *etc.*

| che io | sia | abbia |
|--------|--------|----------|
| | sia | abbia |
| | sia | abbia |
| | siamo | abbiamo |
| | siate | abbiate |
| | síano | ábbiano |

### IMPERFECT

that I spoke, believed, finished, *etc.*

| che io | parlassi | credessi | finissi |
|--------|------------|------------|------------|
| *etc.* | parlassi | credessi | finissi |
| | parlasse | credesse | finisse |
| | parlássimo | credéssimo | finíssimo |
| | parlaste | credeste | finiste |
| | parlássero | credéssero | finíssero |

that I were, had, *etc.*

| che io | fossi | avessi |
|--------|----------|-----------|
| | fossi | avessi |
| | fosse | avesse |
| | fóssimo | avéssimo |
| | fóste | aveste |
| | fóssero | avéssero |

## PRESENT PERFECT

che abbia parlato, etc.
che abbia creduto, etc.
che abbia finito, etc.
che sia stato, etc.
che abbia avuto, etc.

## EXERCISE I

Following the model verbs, form the Present and Imperfect Subjunctive of portare, to carry; véndere, to sell; agire, to act.

**71.** The Subjunctive is used mostly in subordinate clauses, after such verbs as **desiderare** (to wish), **sperare** (to hope), **credere, ritenere** (to believe) and phrases of the type **è giusto, necessario, preferibile, inutile che . . .** If the main verb is in the Present, the Subjunctive will be Present too, or Present Perfect when referring to the past. If the main verb is in the Imperfect, the Subjunctive will be Imperfect too. The remaining infrequent cases will be dealt with in §97 and §98. Finally, the Present Subjunctive expresses polite orders and invitations, therefore it is the Imperative for the third person, singular and plural (see also Lesson VIII).

| | |
|---|---|
| **E' giusto che quel ragazzo abbia un premio.** | It is right that that boy should have a prize. |
| **Il generale desidera che pranziate con lui questa sera.** | The general would like you to dine with him tonight. |
| **La signorina sperava che fosse un invito alla buona.** | The young lady hoped that the invitation was an informal one. |
| **Spero che abbiate fatto buon viaggio.** | I hope that you have had a pleasant journey. |
| **La polizia ritiene che la ragazza abbia mentito.** | The police think that the girl lied. |
| **Lei aspetti, per piacere, loro invece véngano con me.** | Would you wait, please, and would you come with me. |
| **Mi dica la verità, capitano.** | Tell me the truth, captain. |

58

1 it is not right that they should leave to me all the boring obs; 2 it would be better if we wrote that report together; 3 the manager thinks that you (*polite*) are the most suitable person to deal with Mr. Brambilla; 4 we hope that the goods have arrived in good condition; 5 my wife wanted the house to be ready before the holidays; 6 I hope you are all keeping well and that you will come to see us soon.

**72.** The Subjunctive is also used after two idiomatic impersonal expressions: **bisogna, occorre che**, which have the same meaning (*it is necessary that*). **Bisogna che** is used very frequently.
Both expressions also introduce Infinitive clauses.

| | |
|---|---|
| **Bisogna che uno di voi avverta gli uomini.** | One of you must warn the men. |
| **Prima di giudicare bisogna capire.** | You have to understand before you can judge. |
| **Bisognava che il denaro gli arrivasse ad ogni costo.** | The money had to get to him at all costs. |
| **Occorre far presto.** | We have to be quick. |
| **Occorre che nessuno si accorga della loro presenza.** | No one must be aware of their presence. |

Whereas the verb **bisognare** is only conjugated impersonally, in the third person singular, **occorrere** is used personally as well:

| | |
|---|---|
| **Occorrono due operai e un técnico.** | Two workmen and one engineer are needed. |
| **Il trápano non occorre.** | The drill is not needed. |

In these examples, **occorre/occorrono** have an equivalent in **è necessario/sono necessari.**

**73.** DISJUNCTIVE PRONOUNS. The main prepositions, **di, a, da, in, con, su, per, tra**, are often used with pronouns; special forms are then required in the singular:

| | | | |
|---|---|---|---|
| me | **me** | us | **noi** |
| you | **te** | you | **voi** |
| him, her | **lui, lei, sé** | them | **loro, sé** |
| it, itself | **esso, essa, sé** | | |

| | |
|---|---|
| **Abbiamo passato una mezz'ora con lui.** | We spent half an hour with him. |
| **La poltrona è per te.** | The armchair is for you. |
| **Per sé Teresa ha comprato una collana veneziana.** | Teresa bought a Venetian necklace for herself. |
| **Andate da loro.** | Go to them. |
| **Cercate il baule; dentro di esso sono custoditi documenti importanti.** | Look for the chest; some important documents are kept in it. |
| **E' una porta automatica, si chiude da sé.** | The door is automatic, it locks itself. |

**74.** Disjunctive pronouns are also used to convey emphasis. In this case the verb is either understood or comes before the pronoun.

| | |
|---|---|
| **Vuole te, solo te.** | He wants you, only you. |
| **Andiamo noi a cercare i compagni.** | We shall look for our mates. |

## EXERCISE III

1 you must ask them;   2 they won't tell you anything;   3 do you need anything, doctor?;   4 I must phone my brother George at once;   5 why him?;   6 if you need any native porters, let me know;   7 the parents left the big apartment to their son and kept the small one for themselves.

**75.** *Himself, themselves*, etc., used with prepositions, become **sé**, as we have seen. **Sé** is sometimes reinforced by the adjective **stesso** and is written then without the accent.

| | |
|---|---|
| **Odiava se stessa per quello che aveva fatto.** | She hated herself for what she had done. |
| **E' un motivo valido per se stesso.** | It is a good enough reason in itself. |

An important point to remember is that *himself*, *itself*, etc., are used much more frequently in English than **se stesso**, etc. in Italian. Their function is fulfilled, to a great extent, by Reflexive verbs and pronouns which are explained in the next Lesson.

## CONVERSATION

Se non ha fretta di tornare in albergo, signora, la invito a bere qualcosa al Caffè Meletti[1].

If you are not in a hurry to go back to the hotel, madam, I will invite you for a drink at the Cafe Meletti.

Lei è molto gentile. Non ho fretta e mi siederò volentieri perché ho camminato molto, questa mattina.

How kind of you. I am not in a hurry and I will be glad to sit down, because I did a lot of walking this morning.

Va bene questo tavolino? O preferisce quello, all'ombra? Di là potrà vedere sia la gente, sia l'insieme della piazza.

Is this table all right for you? Maybe you prefer the other one in the shade. From there you will be able to watch the people and the whole of the piazza at the same time.

Va bene il tavolino all'ombra. Lei ha ragione, star seduti qui è come essere a teatro!

The table in the shade will be fine. You are quite right: to be sitting here is just like being at the theatre!

In molte città italiane, il caffè sulla piazza principale è ancora un ritrovo e un trattenimento.

In many Italian towns the cafe in the main piazza is still a meeting place and an entertainment.

---

1. Producers of a fine anis liqueur, in a town called Ascoli Piceno.

61

# LESSON FOURTEEN

**76.** REFLEXIVE VERBS. They form a large section of Italian verbs. 'Reflexive' means that the subject is also the object of the action expressed. Objective pronouns are therefore used throughout and must not be omitted. In compound tenses the auxiliary is always **essere**.

divertirsi,    to enjoy oneself
servirsi,    to help oneself

| | |
|---|---|
| I help myself | mi servo |
| you have enjoyed yourself | ti sei divertito |
| he helps himself | si serve |
| she helps herself | |
| we have enjoyed ourselves | ci siamo divertiti |
| are you enjoying yourselves? | vi divertite? |
| they help themselves | si sérvono |
| help yourself! | sérviti! |

Here is a list of the most common reflexive verbs:

| | |
|---|---|
| svegliarsi | to wake up |
| alzarsi | to get up |
| lavarsi | to get washed |
| pettinarsi | to comb one's hair |
| vestirsi | to get dressed |
| cambiarsi | to get changed |
| coricarsi | to lie down, go to bed |
| scusarsi | to apologise |

## EXERCISE I

1 I always wake up early;   2 at what time do you get up?; 3 Ann is washing;   4 we comb our hair again before lunch; 5 get dressed and get out;   6 models change quickly;   7 Robert went to bed last;   8 we apologise for the mistake.

VOCABULARY: model, **indossatrice** f.

**77.** Notice the following sentences:

| | |
|---|---|
| **Il dottore si lava le mani.** ('si' = 'a se stesso') | The doctor is washing his hands. |
| **Ci caricammo le valigie sulle spalle.** ('ci' = 'a noi stessi') | We loaded the cases on our shoulders. |

Where the object is 'le mani' and 'le valigie', **si** and **ci** are only indirect pronouns. In these and many other cases, therefore, the verb is conjugated as reflexive when it is really not. Also note that in the above examples there is an English possessive adjective which disappears in Italian.

**78.** In the examples that follow, the verbs are only apparently reflexive, and express rather a reciprocated action:

| | |
|---|---|
| **I giocatori si lanciavano la palla.** | The players threw the ball to one another. |
| **Tu e tua sorella vi abbracciate raramente.** | You and your sister seldom embrace. |

**79.** Again, sentences are only apparently reflexive when the pronoun before the verb is neither a direct nor an indirect object. It is merely part of the verb and this ought to be called a prenominal verb. The two sentences below illustrate this point, and a list of the more common 'pronominal' verbs follows:

| | |
|---|---|
| **Non mi vergogno di quello che ho fatto.** | I am not ashamed for what I have done. |
| **Il museo si trova presso la cattedrale.** | The museum is near the cathedral. |

| | |
|---|---|
| provarsi | to try |
| sforzarsi | to try hard |
| sedersi | to sit down |
| ricordarsi | to remember |
| ammalarsi | to get ill |
| sbagliarsi | to make a mistake |
| ripetersi | to happen again |
| preoccuparsi | to worry |

Many verbs in both lists can also be used as active verbs, with a different meaning, for instance:

| | |
|---|---|
| **alzare** | to lift |
| ~~cambiare~~ | ~~to become different~~ |
| **provare** | to taste, to try on |
| **trovare** | to find |

## EXERCISE II

1 Blanche has forgotten to buy some cigarettes; 2 if she smokes that much all the time she will get ill; 3 sit down and tell us from the beginning; 4 the alpinist was climbing the rock with ease; 5 if you don't try to play better than this, there is no point continuing training; 6 don't worry, the damages caused by the rain are not serious.

VOCABULARY: cigarette, **sigaretta** *f*; to smoke, **fumare**; beginning, **principio** *m*; alpinist, **alpinista** *m & f*; rock, **roccia** *f*; ease, **facilità** *f*; no point, **inutile**; to continue, **continuare**; training (noun), **allenamento** *m*.

**80.**     **In questo paese si chiacchiera troppo.**
**Si mangia bene da Rosina.**

mean, as you have guessed,

People talk too much in this village.
One eats well at Rosie's.

**Si parla, si mangia** are not reflexive forms (3rd person sing.), for lack of a definite subject and of an object. **Si** can therefore be considered an indefinite subject pronoun; it can also replace, mainly in the spoken language, the first person plural (**noi**):

| | |
|---|---|
| **Ora smettiamo di lavorare e** | = **Si smette di lavorare e si** |
| **andiamo a lavarci.** | **va a lavarsi.** |
| **Parlavamo del più e del** | = **Si parlava del più e del** |
| **meno.** | **meno.** |

Now we shall stop working and get washed.
We were talking about this and that.

64

**81.** Apart from *one* = **si**, there are many indefinite pronouns in Italian, some of which have already been used. Normally the same word can be both pronoun and adjective, and as such can accompany nouns, therefore there can be four endings: **-o, -a, -i, -e**.

| | |
|---|---|
| alcuni/e | some; a few |
| altro; un altro | other; another |
| qualcuno, qualcosa | somebody, someone, |
|    qualche cosa |    something |
| ognuno, ogni cosa, tutto | everybody, everyone, |
| |    everything |
| chiunque | anybody, anyone |
| qualunque cosa | anything |
| nessuno/a | nobody, no one, no, any |
| niente, nulla | nothing |
| parecchi/ie | several, many |
| tutto/i/a/e | all |

In negative sentences, *anybody* and *anything* become **nessuno, niente**.

      She did not see anybody   **Non ha visto nessuno**

**82.** *Some, any* are sometimes translated **qualche, qualunque**, which are used only in the singular (see also §27).

| | |
|---|---|
| I have brought some new records. | **Ho portato qualche (-keh) disco nuovo.** |
| Some girl must have forgotten her lipstick. | **Qualche ragazza avrà dimenticato questo rossetto.** |
| Don't worry, any colour will do. | **Non si preoccupi, va bene qualunque colore.** |

## EXERCISE III

1 they have made some of the cakes, the others they have bought; 2 Luigi has something to tell you, Jane; 3 the old man left everything to somebody he hardly knew; 4 give a bowl of rice to everyone; 5 the work is easy, anybody could learn it; 6 I would give anything to be left alone; 7 nobody knew anything; 8 a few soldiers escaped but many were made prisoners.

VOCABULARY: cake, **dolce** *m*; bowl, **scodella** *f*; rice, **riso** *m*; to leave alone, **lasciare in pace**; prisoner, **prigioniero** *m*.

# CONVERSATION

Vedo parecchie ragazze e signore, sedute ai tavolini con i mariti e gli amici. C'è perfino qualche bambino, fra gli adulti.

I can see many girls and ladies sitting at the tables with their husbands and friends. There are even a few children among the grown-ups.

Certamente. Nelle città, piccole e grandi, le donne frequentano abitualmente i caffè. Non sono esclusi neanche i bambini e i ragazzi, che bévono bevande analcóliche o mangiano gelati. A propósito, lei cosa prende?

Certainly. In the towns and cities it is normal for a woman to go to a cafe. Children and teen-agers are welcome; they have soft drinks or ice-cream. By the way, what will you have?

Acqua brillante ghiacciata con un po' di gin e limone, grazie.

Chilled tonic water with a drop of gin and lemon, please.

Benissimo. Io prenderò una birra. Cameriere!

Very well. I will have a beer. Waiter!

Ho visto il conto che il cameriere ha portato con il vassoio e mi sembra un'esagerazione!

I saw the bill that the waiter brought with the tray of glasses. It seems enormous to me!

Ah Ah! Cara signora, le cose buone si pagano. Il conto comprende il servizio al tavolo, e questo è il primo caffè della città, che ha prezzi un po' più alti. Ma chi beve al banco paga molto di meno, non lo sapeva?

Ah Ah! My dear lady, one has to pay for the good things in life. Service is included in the bill; besides, this is the best cafe in town, where prices are a bit higher. Customers who drink at the bar pay much less, didn't you know?

66

# LESSON FIFTEEN

## 83. PAST DEFINITE

| I spoke, *etc.* | I believed, *etc.* | I finished, *etc.* |
|---|---|---|
| parlái | credéi* | finíi |
| parlasti | credesti | finisti |
| parlò | credé* | finì |
| parlammo | credemmo | finimmo |
| parlaste | credeste | finiste |
| parlárono | credérono* | finírono |

*Note that in the second conjugation there are alternative endings to credéi, credé and credérono: credetti, credette, credéttero.

| I was, *etc.* | I had, *etc.* |
|---|---|
| fúi | ebbi |
| fosti | avesti |
| fu | ebbe |
| fummo | avemmo |
| foste | aveste |
| fúrono | ébbero |

Although this tense (which refers to distant and completed events) belongs mainly to the written language, including journalism, in Central and Southern Italy it is used also conversationally. A difference is then made by speakers between recent and distant events (see also Lesson Six).

| | |
|---|---|
| A few soldiers escaped. | **Alcuni soldati fuggirono.** |
| The presidential aircraft landed exactly at the time scheduled. | **L'aereo presidenziale atterrò in perfetto orario.** |
| What did they tell you in hospital? | **Che ti díssero all'ospedale ?** (South) |
| | **Che ti hanno detto all'ospedale ?** (North) |

## EXERCISE I

1 those were hard years for the young couple;   2 their first child did not go to school until she was ten;   3 the mother, who was a teacher, taught her to read and write;   4 when the new wine was ready a dealer came and bought the lot;   5 we only had left the amount that the family needed;   6 the chairman of our company was seated next to the mayor's wife.

VOCABULARY: hard, **duro**; year, **anno** *m*; couple, **coppia** *f*; to teach, **insegnare**; wine, **vino** *m*; dealer, **negoziante** *m*; the lot, **tutto** (*lit.*: **la partita** *f*); to have left, **rimanere a uno**; amount, **quantità** *f*; chairman, **presidente** *m*; company, **società** *f*; mayor, **sindaco** *m*.

**84.** The PASSIVE VOICE is formed with the auxiliary **essere** and the past participle. So far, Italian resembles English, but while in English the past participle never varies, in Italian it agrees with the subject in gender and number:

| | |
|---|---|
| The house was sold. | **La casa fu venduta.** |

The past participle can have therefore the usual four endings, -o, -a, -i, -e.

| | |
|---|---|
| Raw materials are imported. | **Le materie prime sono importate.** |
| Manufactured products are exported | **I prodotti industriali sono esportati.** |
| The balance was paid by draft. | **Il saldo fu pagato a mezzo tratta.** |

**85.** The first two examples in the above paragraph could have another wording in Italian, while the meaning is unchanged:

**Si importano materie prime.**
**Si esportano prodotti industriali.**

These sentences only look active, in fact their meaning is passive, as we have seen; **si** is not the impersonal **si** of §80 and is called 'si passivante'.

The following phrases also fall into this pattern:

| | |
|---|---|
| **Si parla inglese.** | English spoken. |
| **Si vende** (*or* **véndesi**). | To be sold, for sale. |
| **Si riparano gomme.** | Tyres repaired. |

## EXERCISE II

1 in this area land can be bought cheap;   2 the park was sold;
3 several small villas can now be seen on its grounds;   4 we
promise that a new hospital and the library shall be built;   5 the
people who live in the village have been deceived;   6 the
promise was not kept.

VOCABULARY: land, **terreni** *m. pl.*, **terra** *f*; cheap, **a poco prezzo**;
park, **parco** *m*; ground, **terreno** *m*, on its g. = **al suo posto**; to promise,
**prométtere**; to deceive, **ingannare**; to keep, **mantenere**.

**86.**   Irregular Verbs of the Third Conjugation.

### Infinitive

| uscire, *to go out* | salire, *to go up* | venire, *to come* |
|---|---|---|

### Present

| | | |
|---|---|---|
| esco | salgo | vengo |
| esci | sali | vieni |
| esce | sale | viene |
| usciamo | saliamo | veniamo |
| uscite | salite | venite |
| éscono | salgono | véngono |

Past Participle: uscito; salito; venuto.

**87.**   **Venire** is an important verb, as several other verbs derive
from it and are conjugated in the same way:

| | |
|---|---|
| **avvenire** | to happen |
| **divenire** | to become |
| **prevenire** | to forestall |
| **provenire** | to come from |

**Venire** also has a special function as an alternative auxiliary
in the passive voice:

| | |
|---|---|
| Il vino bianco viene servito ghiacciato. | White wine is served chilled. |
| Le mele vengono suddivise secondo la grossezza. | Apples are graded according to their size. |

## EXERCISE III

1 the road that goes up to the Great St Bernard is wide and comfortable; 2 I have already been out, why don't you go out?; 3 Bruno and Teresa had become his best friends; 4 things like that happen for precise reasons; 5 the painting that you are admiring comes from the Villa Fóscari; 6 Grandma has gone up to her room to rest; 7 the tulips have not come out well.

VOCABULARY: tulip, **tulipano** *m*; precise, **preciso**; reason, **ragione** *f*.

## CONVERSATION

Vorrei due biglietti.
Interi o ridotti?

Two tickets, please.
Ordinary (*lit.* whole price) or half price (*lit.* reduced)?

Ridotti, naturalmente, se si può.
Se siete studenti e avete il tesserino, avete diritto alla riduzione.

Half price, of course, if possible.
If you are students and have your cards, you are entitled to pay half price.

Ecco le nostre téssere. Quanto costa il biglietto a prezzo ridotto?

These are our cards. How much is it, at half price?

La metà, 150 lire invece di 300.

150 lire instead of 300.

Bene. Il museo è aperto anche nel pomeriggio, vero?

That is nice. The museum is open in the afternoon as well, is it not?

No, da quest'anno facciamo l'orario continuato dalle 9 alle 14.

No, we have (are doing) new hours this year, from 9 a.m. until 2 p.m.

Ma la nostra guida dice che il museo è aperto dalle 10 all'una e dalle 3 alle 6, ed è chiuso il lunedì.

My book, though, says that this museum opens from 10 a.m. to 1 p.m. and from 3 p.m. to 6 p.m., and is closed on Mondays.

Era così fino all'anno scorso, adesso facciamo l'orario continuato, come la maggior parte dei musei nazionali. Il lunedì siamo chiusi.

It was like that until last year, now we close at 2 o'clock, like most national museums. We are closed on Mondays.

# LESSON SIXTEEN

**88.** In this lesson, the conjugation of the irregular verbs studied so far will be completed. **Fare** (*to do*) will not be found here but in the following lesson.

A few points should be kept in mind:

(i) the endings of each tense are the same, whether the verb is regular or irregular (it is in the stem that the irregularity occurs);

(ii) the future and the conditional are formed from the same stem;

(iii) the past definite is the tense that may differ most from the infinitive;

(iv) the present subjunctive is similar to the present indicative and it has only one form for the three singular persons;

(v) the imperative is the same as the present tense.

**89.**

| IMPERFECT | FUTURE and CONDITIONAL | |
|---|---|---|
| davo, davamo | darò | darei |
| stavo, stavamo | starò | starei |
| andavo, andavamo | andrò | andrei |
| volevo, volevamo | vorrò | vorrei |
| potevo, potevamo | potrò | potrei |
| dovevo, dovevamo | dovrò | dovrei |
| sapevo, sapevamo | saprò | saprei |
| salivo, salivamo | salirò | salirei |
| uscivo, uscivamo | uscirò | uscirei |
| venivo, venivamo | verrò | verrei |

PAST DEFINITE

diedi, desti, diede; demmo, deste, diédero
stetti, stesti, stette; stemmo, steste, stéttero
andai, andasti, andò; andammo, andaste, andárono

volli, volesti, volle; volemmo, voleste, vóllero
potéi, potesti, poté; potemmo, poteste, potérono
dovéi, dovesti, dové; dovemmo, doveste, dovérono
seppi, sapesti, seppe; sapemmo, sapeste, séppero

71

salii, salisti, salì; salimmo, saliste, salírono
uscii, uscisti, uscì; uscimmo, usciste, uscírono
venni, venisti, venne; venimmo, veniste, vénnero

| PRESENT SUBJUNCTIVE | IMPERFECT SUBJUNCTIVE |
|---|---|
| dia, díano (that I, they give) | dessi, deste, déssero (that I, you *pol.*, they give) |
| stia, stíano | stessi, steste, stéssero |
| vada, andiamo, andiate, vádano | andassi, andaste, andássero |
| voglia, vógliano | volessi, voleste, voléssero |
| possa, póssano | potessi, poteste, potéssero |
| debba, dobbiamo, dobbiate, débbano | dovessi, doveste, dovéssero |
| sappia, sáppiano | sapessi, sapeste, sapéssero |
| salga, saliamo, salgano | salissi, saliste, salíssero |
| esca, usciamo, usciate, éscano | uscissi, usciste, uscíssero |
| venga, veniamo, veniate, véngano | venissi, veniste, veníssero |

GERUND

| dando | volendo | salendo |
|---|---|---|
| stando | potendo | uscendo |
| andando | dovendo | venendo |
| | sapendo | |

## EXERCISE I

1 they knew;  2 you had to;  3 he wanted;  4 you will stay;  5 you (*pl*) will know;  6 they will be able;  7 they could;  8 you will go out;  9 you (*pl*) would go out;  10 we shall come;  11 we would come;  12 we would;  13 go (*pl*);  14 you (*pl*) will go;  15 go out;  16 come.

72

## EXERCISE II

1 what if I went?; 2 what if they came?; 3 it is better for you to know; 4 it was time for us to go up; 5 it is time for him to go up; 6 if he had to give the key, he would give it; 7 he could betray you if he wanted to; 8 whether he wants it or not, my brother will have to give me the money; 9 as I shall be visiting your city I thought I would write to you.

VOCABULARY: to betray, **tradire**; to visit, **recarsi, visitare.**

## LESSON SEVENTEEN

**90.** **Fare** (see §50) does not really belong to the first conjugation, as it is a contracted form from **fácere**. The stem **fac-** appears in the present and imperfect tenses, in the gerund, in the others the letter **-c-** is dropped and the form that results from this is a shortened or contracted one.

The same pattern returns in two very frequent verbs: **dire** (*to say*, *to tell*), and **bere** (*to drink*), contracted from **dícere** and **bévere.**

PRESENT INDICATIVE

faccio (see §50)
dico, dici, dice, diciamo, dite, dícono
bevo, bevi, beve, beviamo, bevete, bévono

IMPERFECT

facevo, facevi, faceva, facevamo, facevate, facévano
dicevo, dicevi, diceva, dicevamo, dicevate, dicévano
bevevo, bevevi, beveva, bevevamo, bevevate, bevévano

PAST DEFINITE

feci, facesti, fece, facemmo, faceste, fécero
dissi, dicesti, disse, dicemmo, diceste, díssero
bevvi, bevesti, bevve, bevemmo, beveste, bévvero

73

| FUTURE | CONDITIONAL |
|---|---|
| farò, farai, *etc.* | farei, faresti, *etc.* |
| dirò, dirai, *etc.* | direi, diresti, *etc.* |
| berrò, berrai, *etc.* | berrei, berresti, *etc.* |

| PRESENT SUBJUNCTIVE | IMPERFECT SUBJUNCTIVE |
|---|---|
| faccia, facciamo | facessi, facéssimo |
| dica, diciamo | dicessi, dicéssimo |
| beva, beviamo | bevessi, bevéssimo |

PAST PARTICIPLE: fatto — detto — bevuto.

GERUND: facendo — dicendo — bevendo.

There are about 150 irregular verbs in Italian, plus their derivatives. In this book you will not find complete tables of verbs; dictionaries will be helpful, but we recommend especially Hugo's little book *Italian Verbs Simplified*.


## EXERCISE I

1 why do you say so?   2 we say these things because they are true;   3 drink this medicine, it will do you good;   4 the sailor drank;   5 what would you say about a walk after dinner?; 6 I am afraid it will be cold;   7 if it is cold we shall put our coats ('a coat') on; 8 the survivors told that it had been an awful retreat;   9 the captain was doing his report.

VOCABULARY: sailor, **marinaio** *m*; coat, **giacca** *f*; survivor, **superstite** *m*; awful, **spaventoso**; retreat, **ritirata**, *f*.
NOTE how in Italian idiom *our coats* becomes *a coat*.


**91.** Some regular verbs of the first conjugation which end in **-care, -gare** show a peculiarity that must be noted: an **h** is added before any **i** or **e** in order to maintain the stem sound throughout. In fact, **chi** and **ghi** sound *kee* and *guee*, but **ci** and **gi** sound *see* and *jee*. For example, take **giocare**, *to play*.

| PRESENT INDICATIVE | SUBJUNCTIVE |
|---|---|
| gioco | giochi |
| giochi | giochi |
| gioca | giochi |
| giochiamo | giochiamo |
| giocate | giochiate |
| giócano | gióchino |

| FUTURE | CONDITIONAL |
|---|---|
| giocherò | giocherei |
| giocherai | giocheresti |
| giocherà | giocherebbe |
| giocheremo | giocheremmo |
| giocherete | giochereste |
| giocheranno | giocherébbero |

With **navigare** (*to sail*) it is exactly the same: **návighi, navighiamo, návighino**; **navigherò**; **navigherei**, etc.

Here is a list of some frequent verbs of this type:

| | |
|---|---|
| sporcare, to soil | annegare, to drown |
| medicare, to cure | indagare, to investigate |
| stancarsi, to get tired | pregare, to pray, beg |
| imbarcarsi, to get on board | fregare, to wipe. |

Some other regular verbs show alterations of the stem in a few tenses. Since these alterations affect the written rather than the spoken language, they will be explained in the Appendix.

**92.** 'All he said' and 'all I did' become in Italian

tutto quello che ha detto
tutto quello che ho fatto,

**quello che** being the demonstrative+relative pronoun tha must not be divided.

**93.** 'I wonder' is a common English expression which is rer dered in several ways. The meaning, of course, will b slightly different each time.

| I wonder whether Ann understood. | —Chissà (who knows) se Anna ha capito. |
| | —Avrà capito, Anna ? |
| | —Mi domando se Anna ha capito. |
| | —Vorrei sapere se Anna ha capito. |
| I wonder when the parcel will come. | —Chissà quando arriverà il pacco. |
| | —Quando arriverà, il pacco ? |
| | —Mi domando quando arriverà il pacco. |
| | —Vorrei sapere quando arriverà il pacco. |
| I wonder who (or how he) took the car. | —Chissà chi (come) ha preso la macchina. |
| | —Chi (come) avrà preso la macchina ? |
| | —Mi domando chi (come) ha preso la macchina. |
| | —Vorrei sapere chi (come) ha preso la macchina. |

The future perfect, in the above examples, expresses uncertainty.

## EXERCISE II

1 all the doctor said is that the patient's condition is nothing to worry about;   2 send us enough supplies, that's all we ask for;   3 I wonder how long the four men will still keep it up for;   4 I wonder when it will stop raining;   5 I wonder whether Roger will get his driving licence today;   6 the judge wanted to know whether those words really were all the defendant had said on the evening of the 18th.

VOCABULARY: nothing to worry about, **non destare preoccupazioni**; supplies, **rifornimenti** *m*; to keep it up, **resistere**; to stop, **smettere di**; to get a driving licence, **prendere la patente**; judge, **ǵiúdice**, *m*; defendant, **imputato** *m*.

**94.** *As far as I* (or *we*) *know* becomes

> per quanto ne sappia io (ne sappiamo noi) *or*
> per quello che ne so io (ne sappiamo noi);

the subjunctive is used in the first expression.

76

| As far as we know, the ship left Singapore on the 15th. | Per quanto ne sappiamo noi, la nave ha lasciato Singapore il 15. |
| As far as Mr. Moro knows, Miss Moro is still in New York. | Per quello che ne sa il signor Moro, la signorina Moro è ancora a New York. |

**95.** *No sooner . . .,* and *as soon as* become **non appena**, used as follows:

| No sooner had she got the money than she bought herself a camera. | Non appena ebbe il denaro essa si comprò una macchina fotografica. |
| As soon as they hear from Vincent they will phone his family | Non appena avranno notizie di Vincenzo telefoneranno alla sua famiglia. |

**96.** Compare *a time when, a place where* with

**un luogo in cui, un momento in cui**

The same structure, **in + cui**, is used for both time and place. You may have expected **quando** and **dove** to be used and in fact **dove** can be used; **quando** cannot:

| There is a time when all the flowers have gone. | Viene un momento in cui non ci sono più fiori. |
| There must be a place where people like him met to have a good time. | Ci doveva essere un posto in cui le persone come lui si incontravano per divertirsi. |

## EXERCISE III

1 this is the square where they are waiting;   2 the only evening when we are both in is Friday;   3 I wonder whether my sister-in-law will give me back those 10,000 lire which I lent her; 4 as far as we know Vanna is all right;   5 as soon as she pays me I will let you know.

VOCABULARY: to lend **imprestare;** the only, **l'unico;** to be all right, **essere** (una donna) **a posto.**

77

# CONVERSATION

All'angolo di questa strada c'è stato un incidente. Hanno investito un uomo.

There has been an accident at the corner of the road. A man has been knocked down.

Non mi stupisce. In quel punto ci dovrebbero essere le strisce pedonali.

I'm not surprised. They should put a zebra crossing there.

Non farebbero nessuna differenza. Quando la gente si ritrova un volante fra le mani, diventa come matta.

That wouldn't change anything. Once people get behind a steering wheel they become maniacs.

Sciocchezze. Riconosco che le automobili sono pericolose ma trovo che la maggior parte degli automobilisti sono prudenti.

Nonsense. I admit that cars are dangerous but I think most drivers are sensible.

Ma che dici! Gli automobilisti sono terribilmente sbadati. Ieri ho visto un uomo che facendo marcia indietro è andato a finire contro un albero. E se fosse stata una persona anziana?

Go on! Drivers are terribly careless. Yesterday I saw a man back into a tree. It could have been an old woman.

Si possono commettere molti errori, lo so, perché quando uno guida deve pensare a tante cose, e si dimentica. E' come se la macchina diventasse parte del guidatore. Non pensiamo mica a dove mettiamo la forchetta quando mangiamo, no?

I know that they make a lot of mistakes, but that is because there are so many things to think about when driving—and people forget. It is as though the car became part of themselves. You don't think about where you are putting your fork when you are eating, do you?

## LESSON EIGHTEEN

**97.** SUBJUNCTIVE CLAUSES. They are generally introduced by a word formed with the conjunction **che**, joining them to the main clause. Such words are: perché, affinché, purché, benché, sebbene, senza che.

| | |
|---|---|
| **Chiudono le persiane perché non entri troppa luce.** | They closed the shutters so that too much light should not enter. |
| **Una minoranza combatté affinché il paese fosse liberato dagli stranieri.** | A minority fought in order to free the country from all foreigners. |
| **Il vecchio gli perdonerebbe, purché il figlio tornasse da lui.** | The old man would forgive provided that the son went back to him. |
| **Benché (sebbene) abbiate tanti soldi, siete scontenti.** | Although you have lots of money, you are not satisfied. |
| **Giuseppe è venuto senza che lo chiamassero.** | Joseph came without having been called. |

**98.** Many subjunctive clauses are introduced by **se** (*if*), expressing a circumstance that did not materialize:

| | |
|---|---|
| **Se l'avessi saputo!** | If I had known! |
| **Se il dottore avesse ordinato una medicina, l'avremmo comprata subito.** | If the doctor had prescribed a medicine we would have bought it at once. |

In different situations **se** introduces the present indicative and the future:

| | |
|---|---|
| **Se ci vai tu, ci vado anch'io.** | If you go, I will go too. |
| **Se suo fratello verrà a casa vostra ci starà almeno una settimana.** | If his brother is going to stay with you, he will stay a week at least. |

The above clauses are common even in spoken Italian. There are ways of avoiding them, if you don't feel too sure, by simplifying your sentences. The second and fourth examples in §97, for instance, can be simplified thus:

**Il vecchio gli perdonerebbe, ma il figlio deve tornare da lui.**
**Giuseppe è venuto senza essere stato chiamato.**

79

# EXERCISE I

1 we shut the windows so that the mosquitoes will not get in; 2 although he had gone into a difficult profession Edmund grew rich; 3 the boy was prepared to accept any sacrifice provided they allowed him to study the violin; 4 the town had expanded and we had not noticed; 5 if the train had been two minutes late we would have caught it; 6 I have asked you to come so that you could meet Peter, my American brother; 7 let the people say what they like, I'll suit myself.

VOCABULARY: to shut, **chiúdere**; window, **finestra** *f*; mosquito, **zanzara** (dsan-dsah-rah) *f*; profession, **professione** *f*; to go into, **esercitare**; to grow rich, **diventare ricco**; sacrifice, **sacrificio** *m*; to allow, **lasciare**; violin, **violino** (vee-oh-lee-noh) *m*; to expand, **créscere**; to notice, **accórgersi**; to catch, **préndere**; to let, **lasciare**; to suit oneself, **fare quel che (gli) pare**.

99. **Poco** and **molto** are an interesting couple of words, of opposite meaning and similar behaviour:

| | |
|---|---|
| C'è poco tempo. | There is little time. |
| C'è molto tempo. | There is plenty of time. |
| Vedo pochi uccelli. | I can see few birds. |
| Vedo molti uccelli. | I can see many birds. |
| È venuta poca gente. | Few people came. |
| Abbiamo portato molta roba. | We brought lots of things. |
| Renzo viaggia poco. | Renzo does not travel much. |
| | Renzo does little travelling. |
| | Renzo is not a great traveller. |
| Renzo viaggia molto. | Renzo travels a lot. |

The last examples are particularly interesting because they cover several English possibilities. Finally, notice

| | |
|---|---|
| Sarà vero, ma ci credo poco. | It may be true, still I don't believe it. |

**Poco**, as an adverb, is often shortened to **po'**; followed by **di**, it means 'a little amount of'; it is also used idiomatically, expressing concern or curiosity:

| | |
|---|---|
| Vieni un po' qui . . . | Come here a moment . . . |
| Di' un po', cosa voleva da te quel tale ? | Tell me, what did that fellow want from you? |
| Dateci ancora un po' di tempo. | Give us some more time. |
| Ci vorrebbe un po' di sole. | What we want is a little sunshine. |

80

Notice the idioms

| siete in pochi, in molti | there are few, many of you |
| sono in tre, in cinque | there are three, five of them |

## 100. *Not much* becomes **non molto**, or **non . . . un gran che**:

| Did you enjoy yourself? | **Ti sei divertito ?** |
| Not much. | **Non molto.** |
| The market was big but we didn't buy much. | **Il mercato era grande ma non abbiamo comprato gran che.** |

## EXERCISE II

1 there are many huntsmen but little game;   2 the youth had been to the cinema only a few times;   3 we have little money and we would like an inexpensive room;   4 with a little patience the job will turn out quite well;   5 the old man had told little, nevertheless that little enabled the journalist to understand many things;   6 there were many of us catching the ferry to Messina.

VOCABULARY: huntsman, **cacciatore** (kah-chah-tor-eh) *m*; game, **selvaggina** *f*; youth, **gióvane** *m*; cinema (chée-ne-mah) *m*; inexpensive, **che non costa molto**; patience, **pazienza** (pah-tsien-tsa) *f*; to turn out, **venire**; nevertheless, **ma**; to enable, **permettere**; to catch, **prendere**; ferry, **traghetto** *m*.

## 101. **Tutto, tutti** (see §81) are also adjectives and translate both *all* and *whole*; they reinforce other adjectives as well:

| **Tutto il mondo.** | The whole world. |
| **Ha venduto tutte le camicette.** | He sold all the blouses. |
| **Ha macchiato tutta la camicetta.** | She stained the blouse all over. |
| **Abbiamo riesaminato tutti i conti.** | We have checked the accounts all over. |
| **Era tutta frádicia.** | She was soaking wet. |

As pronouns, **tutto/i** mean everything, everybody as well as all:

| **Erano tutti contenti.** | Everybody was happy. |
| **Pietro ha venduto tutto quello che aveva.** | Peter sold everything he had. |

81

**102.** The last example and the word 'everything' can acquire slightly different meanings which in Italian become:

| | |
|---|---|
| **Ha venduto ogni cosa.** | He sold every single thing. |
| **Ogni oggetto fu imballato con cura.** | Everything was carefully packed. |
| **Ogni giorno il bambino studiava il pianoforte per un'ora.** | The child practised the piano for an hour every day. |

## EXERCISE III

1 I have a friend who knows all the pop songs; 2 one evening he hears a new song and the following day he knows it all already; 3 he knows everything, of course, about every singer and musician; 4 he likes nothing better than listening to his favourite bands; 5 his brothers don't understand him; 6 it is normal, people don't all have the same tastes.

VOCABULARY: pop song, **canzone** *f* (cahn-tso-neh) **in voga**; to hear, **sentire**; singer, **cantante** *m*; musician, **musicista** (moo-zee-chee-stah); to like nothing better than, **il maggior divertimento è di . . .**; taste, **gusto** *m*.

## CONVERSATION

Vado a fare due passi. Vuoi venire anche tu?

I am going out for a short walk. Do you want to come?

Non ho voglia di uscire, sto bene qui.

I don't feel like going out, I am all right where I am.

Veramente neanch'io ne ho molta voglia, ma non si può stare in casa tutto il giorno.

I don't really feel like it myself, but one can't stay in all day.

Che gusto ci provi a uscire con questo freddo? La strada sarà piena di pozzánghere e di fango.

What pleasure do you get in going out in this cold? The road must be full of mud and puddles.

Non esagerare, non è piovuto tanto forte. Se hai paura di qualche pozzanghera e di un po' di fango, méttiti gli stivali di gomma come ho fatto io. L'aria fresca ti farà passare il cattivo umore.

Don't exaggerate, it did not rain all that much. If you fear the puddles and the mud put on your wellingtons, as I did. The fresh air will get rid of your bad mood.

# LESSON NINETEEN

**103.** In English *to* is the only preposition to be found before an infinitive; the other prepositions are followed by the gerund, e.g.

*by stopping, from burning, for baking.*

In Italian, as we have already seen (§64), the gerund is used without a preposition, while the infinitive can be used either on its own (*essa guarda le lettere bruciare*) or with any preposition following another verb, a noun or an adjective. The infinitive in Italian is therefore used almost as a noun.

At the beginning it is necessary to study these usages, then they will gradually become familiar to you.

## INFINITIVE WITHOUT PREPOSITION

| | |
|---|---|
| **Ruggero preferisce aspettare nell'ingresso.** | Roger prefers to wait in the hall. |
| **Teresa non osava alzare gli occhi.** | Teresa dared not look up. |
| **Lascia fare a me.** | Let me do it, leave it to me. |
| **Dal balcone vi furono saluti e uno sventolare di fazzoletti.** | From the balcony came calls and waving of handkerchiefs. |
| (*In narrations*) | |
| **... e la domenica mattina fare il bucato, portare a spasso i ragazzi nel pomeriggio ...** | ... doing the washing on Sunday mornings, taking the children out in the afternoons. |

## WITH 'A'

| | |
|---|---|
| **Gli hanno insegnato a cavalcare.** | They taught him to ride. |
| **Hai cominciato a capire.** | You have begun to understand. |
| **Vado a chiamare il medico.** | I am going to call the doctor. |
| **Lucia si mise a piangere.** | Lucy started to cry. |
| **L'impiegato stette a sentire.** | The clerk listened. |
| **Pronto, disposto a dichiarare.** | Ready, willing to declare. |
| **Utile a sapersi.** | Useful to know. |
| **Il primo, l'ultimo a essere servito.** | The first, the last to be served. |

| | |
|---|---|
| A giudicare dalla pronunzia . . . | Judging from (their) pronunciation . . . |
| A sentir lui, la colpa è tutta degli avversari. | According to him all the blame is to be laid on the opponents. |

*(In narrations)*

| | |
|---|---|
| La folla a batter le mani, a gridare. | The crowd was clapping and shouting. |
| E noi a dire che non era vero nulla. | We kept saying that it was not true at all. |

## WITH 'DI'

| | |
|---|---|
| Ti prego di venire. | I ask you to come. |
| Non dubito di riuscire. | I have no doubt that I shall succeed. |
| Credo di aver ragione. | I think I am right. |
| Ho deciso di provare. | I have decided I shall try. |
| Aspetterò di essere chiamato. | I shall wait until they call me. |
| Mi ha scritto di essere malato. | He wrote to me that he is ill. |
| Il desiderio, la speranza di guarire. | The desire, the hope to recover. |
| La decisione, la volontà di ricominciare. | The decision, the will to start again. |
| Sono contento, sicuro, capace di vincere. | I am glad, sure, capable of winning. |

## WITH 'DA'

| | |
|---|---|
| Portateci da bere. | Bring us something to drink. |
| Non ho nulla da dire. | I don't have anything to say. |
| Abbiamo da lavorare. | We have got work to do. |
| Macchina da cucire, da scrivere. | Sewing machine, typewriter. |
| Casa da vendere. | House for sale. |

## WITH 'PER'

| | |
|---|---|
| Sta per partire. | He is going to leave. |
| Finivano per dargli ragione in tutto (*but also*: finivano col dargli ragione . . .). | They ended up saying he was right about everything. |
| Per voler troppo non ottiene nulla. | By wanting too much he doesn't get anything. |
| Per essere stato in guerra hai poca disinvoltura. | For somebody who has been in the war you are rather awkward. |

84

**104.** The other prepositions which can be used with the Infinitive keep the meaning they would have normally. They are: **senza**; **invece di**; **dopo, dopo di**; **prima di.**
Examples:

| | |
|---|---|
| **La tua collega è andata via senza salutare.** | Your colleague went away without saying good-bye. |
| **Invece di criticare, cercate di capire.** | Instead of criticising, try to understand. |
| **Dopo aver ascoltato il brano, leggetelo a voce alta.** | After listening to the extract read it in a loud voice. |
| **Prima di fare gli esercizi riascolterete il brano.** | Before you do the exercises you will listen to the passage again. |

**105.** **Volere, dovere, potere** (*to want, to have, to to be able to*) are followed immediately by the Infinitive, like this:

| | |
|---|---|
| **Non potevano bere tutte in una volta.** | They could not drink all at the same time. |
| **Dovevano stabilire una specie di turno.** | They had to take turns at it. |
| **Marietta voleva bere per prima.** | Mary wanted to drink first. |

## EXERCISE I

Fill in the gaps with the appropriate prepositions:

'Mi accade abbastanza spesso . . . fare questo sogno. Avere davanti agli occhi una pagina scritta, e doverla leggere. Il tormento non incomincia subito. Leggo qualche linea ma a poco a poco incomincia . . . diventare difficile —— perché sul foglio compaiono non più parole, ma cose. Oggetti: un aratro, una sedia. Eppure io *devo* leggere. Faccio un tremendo sforzo . . . tradurre in parole le cose, ma mancando i nessi non riesco . . . combinare un discorso. Cerco . . . inventare, ma sento sempre più che il senso mi sfugge, mentre tanto più pesano con la loro massiccia evidenza, le cose.'

(*L. Romano*)

**106.** The superlative is formed in Italian with the suffix **-íssimo,** **-íssima, -íssimi, -íssime.** It is used with adjectives and adverbs, thus:

| | |
|---|---|
| finíssimo | very fine |
| beníssimo | very well |

| | |
|---|---|
| **Prese una stoffa finissima e ne fece una sciarpa.** | He took a very fine cloth and made a scarf with it. |
| **Era difficilissimo parlare con il príncipe.** | It was extremely difficult to speak to the prince. |
| **Alì fu ricevuto prestissimo perché aveva la sciarpa.** | Ali was received very soon because of his scarf. |

This superlative is generally used whenever in English an adjective or adverb is accompanied by *extremely, very, very . . . indeed*. For the form 'the finest' see §46.

**107.** MAGGIORE, MINORE. Although literally **maggiore** means *greater, bigger,* as in **Lago Maggiore,** another frequent meaning is *more important*:

| | |
|---|---|
| **La maggiore casa editrice dell'Italia meridionale è Laterza.** | The most important publisher of Southern Italy is Laterza. |
| **Le maggiori scoperte dell'Ottocento.** | The greatest discoveries of the XIXth century. |

**Minore,** on the other hand, means *smaller* and *less important*:

| | |
|---|---|
| **Con il nostro sistema otterrete gli stessi risultati con minor spesa** | With our system you will get the same results with less expense. |
| **Le entrate sono minori del previsto.** | The revenues are smaller than expected. |
| **Il tuo Cósimo Rosselli è un artista minore.** | Your Cósimo Rosselli is a minor artist. |

Both adjectives are used to indicate the age of young people:

| | |
|---|---|
| **Bruno è il maggiore di tutti noi.** | Bruno is the eldest of us children. |
| **Anna è la minore, la maggiore è Teresa.** | Ann is the younger, Teresa is the elder. |

**Maggiorenne, minorenne** derive from the above and mean respectively of age, under age as in

| I minorenni hanno bisogno di un'autorizzazione speciale per sposarsi. | People under age need a special licence to get married. |

**108.** Similar to the above are the other two comparatives

migliore—meglio (*adv*), better
peggiore—peggio (*adv*), worse

There are also special forms, directly derived from Latin, for the four superlatives:

| óttimo | extremely good |
| péssimo | extremely bad |
| mássimo | greatest—the maximum |
| mínimo | smallest—the minimum. |

but one can equally say: **buonissimo, cattivissimo, grandissimo, piccolissimo.**

*The best, the worst* are tendered by **il migliore, il peggiore.**

| Il vino di Mario è migliore di questo; il migliore di tutti però è il vino di Luigi. | Mario's wine is better than this one; the best of all, though, is Luigi's wine. |
| La missione fu compiuta con la massima velocità. | The mission was accomplished extremely quickly. |
| Le pérdite sono minime. | The losses are very small indeed. |
| Siamo capitati in un pessimo albergo; ci andrà meglio domani. | We have ended up in a terrible hotel; we'll do better tomorrow. |

## EXERCISE II

1 Renzo Ricci was an excellent actor, I always went to see him;   2 after the operation he was very weak, very weak indeed; 3 his children went to see him in hospital very often;   4 it is the best hospital in town;   5 there are three very good hospitals, but this one is super;   6 the prevention of illnesses is not less important than the treatment, on the contrary;   7 the average student reads only two books a month, three at the most;

8 there is no greater sorrow than remembering happy times when one is most unhappy.

## CONVERSATION

*Titina.* Ho avuto un telegramma dallo zio Gaetano. Mia madre è gravissima. Ha la broncopolmonite. Devo partire. Come faccio? Con chi lascio i bambini?

I have had a telegram from Uncle Gaetano. My mother has got pneumonia, she is in a very bad way. I must go. What can I do? With whom shall I leave the kids?

*Sofia.* Cì sono io. C'e Perfetta. E c'e anche la segretaria.

I am here. And Perfetta. And the secretary.

*T.* Nessuno che voglia bene ai bambini. Tu te ne infischi. Non hai nessuna tenerezza per i bambini. Perfetta si sa com'e. Un'antipática. Riguardo alla segretaria, l'ho licenziata.

And no one who is fond of the children. You couldn't care less and have no feeling for children. Perfetta, we know what she is like. Quite disagreeable. As for the secretary, I have given her the sack.

*Nino.* L'hai licenziata?

You have sacked her?

*T.* Si. Le avevo detto di preparare il Nestogen. Lo doveva sbattere con la forchetta. L'ha sbattuto male, è venuto tutto a grumi. E poi deve aver sbagliato la dose.

Yes. I had told her to do the Nestogen. She had to beat it with a fork, she did not do it well and it came up all in lumps. She must have used the wrong amount, too.

*N.* Che diritto hai di licenziare le mia segretaria? Non la lascerò andar via. Rimarrà qui. Non è mica un delitto, sbagliare la dose del latte in pólvere.

You have no right to sack my secretary. I will not let her go. She will stay. It isn't a crime to use the wrong amount of milk powder.

88

*T.* Lo dici tu che non è un delitto. E se al bambino gli viene la gastroenterite? Le ho strappato di mano la bottiglia, e ho versato il latte nel lavandino. Le ho detto di andarsene fuori dai piedi. M'ha detto vecchia scema. Io le ho detto vípera. Le ho dato uno schiaffo.

*S.* Non è una vipera, è una lucértola. Un topo.

*T.* Io non so cosa farmene dei topi. Devi darmi dei soldi, Nino. E poi voglio l'orario dei treni. Mia madre è gravissima. Non so se la troverò viva.

You say so! What if the baby develops gastroenteritis? I grabbed the bottle from her and poured the milk in the sink. I told her to get out of my way. She called me silly old woman. I called her viper. I slapped her.

She is not a viper, she is a lizard, or a mouse.

I have no use for mice. You must give me some money, Nino. Also, I want the railway timetable. My mother is in a very bad way. I wonder whether she will still be alive.

(*From* LA SEGRETARIA, *Act I, by N. Ginzburg*)

89

**109.** You have already learnt that nouns in Italian have gender and divide into masculine and feminine. Those referring to things are fixed in their gender (**la scarpa, il cappello**), but nouns indicating persons or animals normally have a masculine and a feminine form. The latter is obtained according to a few rules, apart from the basic **-o/-a** rule.

(*a*) A few nouns ending in **-a** and **-e** add **-essa**:

| | |
|---|---|
| **poeta, poetessa** | poet |
| **dottore, dottoressa** | doctor |
| **professore, professoressa** | teacher, professor |
| **príncipe, principessa** | prince |

(*b*) Some **-e** nouns only change **-e** into **-a**, others do not change at all:

| | |
|---|---|
| **signore, signora** | lord, lady (Mr., Mrs.) |
| **pardone, padrona** | master, mistress |
| **portiere, portiera** | porter |
| **il/la nipote** | grandchild, etc. |
| **il/la francese** | Frenchman, Frenchwoman |

(*c*) The ending **-tore** becomes **-trice**:

| | |
|---|---|
| **direttore, direttrice** | headmaster, mistress; manager |
| **imperatore, imperatrice** | emperor, empress |
| **pittore, pittrice** | painter |

(*d*) Nouns in **-ante, -ente, -ista** do not vary:

| | |
|---|---|
| **il/la cantante** | singer |
| **il/la violinista** | violinist |
| **il/la parente** | relative |

but

**presidente, presidentessa**

(*e*) There are pairs of nouns of different form which indicate pairs of beings:

| | |
|---|---|
| **gallo, gallina** | cock, hen |
| **re, regina** | king, queen |
| **uomo, donna** | man, woman |

90

(*f*) a variety of patterns is to be found where animal names are concerned:

**gatto, gatta**
**cane, cagna**
**elefante, elefantessa**
**il topo maschio, il topo fémmina**
**la tigre maschio, la tigre fémmina**

## EXERCISE I

1 some modern Italian women writers are very interesting; 2 who would have said that Adele would become a good journalist?; 3 the paediatrician (*f*) says that Tommy cannot have any sweets or cakes; 4 a fashion designer earns what she wants; 5 in ancient days there were also women, not only men prophets.

VOCABULARY: paediatrician, **pediatra**; sweets, **caramelle** *f*; fashion designer, **disegnatrice di mode**; ancient days, **antichità** *f*; prophet, **profeta** *m*, **profetessa** *f*.

**110.** In Italian it is possible to modify to a great extent the meaning of a noun, adverb or adjective by means of special endings added to it, for example:

**libro—libretto—librone—libraccio**
**bene—benino—benone**
**allegro—allegretto—allegrone.**

These suffixes are very widely used but they are not compulsory and depend largely on the speaker's (or writer's) mood and intentions. Therefore, one can use adjectives and adverbs instead, thus:

**grosso libro—librone**        **abbastanza bene—benino**
**brutto libro—libraccio**        **molto allegro—allegrone**

At least another ending should be mentioned: **-astro**, which is sometimes used instead of **-accio**:

**giovinastro**   bad youth, a lout
(**librastro** is not used at all, **librino** is rare, but there is **libriccino . . .**)

91

It is better not to use these very idiomatic suffixes if you are not quite sure of their meaning. In particular, it is incorrect to use 'piccolo' with diminutive nouns, such as **bambino**, **casetta**, **quadretto**, etc., although it is perfectly correct to use other adjectives, i.e.

**un povero gattino—una bella casetta—il prezioso quadretto**

## EXERCISE II

Translate the following passages:

"O della tua giacchetta, de' tuoi calzoncini e del tuo berretto che cosa ne hai fatto?"

"Ho incontrato i ladri e mi hanno spogliato. Dite, buon vecchio, non avreste per caso da darmi un po' di vestituccio, tanto perché io possa ritornare a casa?"

"Ragazzo mio, in fatto di vestiti io non ho che un sacchetto, dove ci tengo i lupini. Se vuoi, piglialo: eccolo là."

Pinocchio prese subito il sacchetto dei lupini che era vuoto, e dopo averci fatto colle forbici una piccola buca nel fondo e due buche dalle parti, se lo infilò a uso camicia. E vestito leggerino a quel modo, si avviò verso il paese.

(*C. Collodi*)

"E' molto pessimista, mia madre. E' molto diffidente. Se ne starebbe là, in un angolo, vicino alla finestra, a sorvegliare quei suoi pentolini, spaventata, diffidente, amara, nella sua vestaglietta giapponese, con quel suo codino di capelli attorcigliato in cima alla testa con un elástico nero . . ."

(*N. Ginzburg*)

111. Sometimes a change of gender is brought about by the suffixes we have just seen. It is as though a new word, largely independent, had been created, as in

| *f.* | *m.* |
|---|---|
| **coda**, tail | **codino**, small, thin tail |
| **cesta**, basket | **cestino**, small basket |
| **tavola**, table | **tavolino**, small table; writing table |
| **barca**, boat | **barcone**, long boat |
| **scimmia**, monkey | **scimmiotto**, young monkey |
| **zucca**, pumpkin | **zucchino** (or **zucchina**), courgette |
| **cappa**, cloak | **cappotto**, winter coat |

**112.** A change of gender and meaning may also occur between singular and plural; besides the ordinary plural in -i a few masculine nouns have a feminine plural in -a (derived from the Latin neutral). A list of the most usual ones is given below:

braccio, le braccia, arms
membro, le membra, limbs
gesto, i gesti, gestures
fondamento, fondamenti, basis, ground
urlo, le urla, screams

bracci, wings
membri, members
le gesta, feats
le fondamenta, foundations
gli urli (*when defined by a numeral*)

ciglio, i cigli, edge of eyelid *or* (*fig.*) of road, *etc.*
dito, le dita, fingers
ginocchio, i ginocchi, knees

le ciglia, eyelashes

i diti, fingers
le ginocchia, knees (*in idiomatic expressions*)

uovo, le uova, eggs
frutto, a piece of fruit, product, result (*fig.*)
la frutta, fruit.

*This has no* -i *ending*
i frutti

## CONVERSATION

Vediamo un po' se conoscete la geografia. Mettiamo che andiate a passare qualche giorno sul Lago di Garda: a quale aereoporto vi conviene arrivare, Milano o Venezia?

Let's see if you know your geography. Suppose that you are going to spend a few days on Lake Garda; which airport would you choose, Milan or Venice?

A Milano, direi, perché il Garda è più vicino a Milano che a Venezia.

Milan, I think, because this lake is nearer to Milan than to Venice.

Sì, bene, e possibilmente arrivereste all'aereoporto di Linate, che dista dal centro solo una ventina di minuti.

All right. If possible you would also choose Linate Airport, only twenty minutes away from the centre.

L'altro aereoporto milanese, la Malpensa, non mi ha lasciato un buon ricordo: ci vuole un'ora per arrivare

The other one, Malpensa, recalls unpleasant memories for me: the coach takes an hour to get to the Porta

93

al terminal di Porta Garibaldi e il pullmann costa caro, 1500 lire.

Andiamo avanti. Arrivati a Milano, come si fa per andare al Lago di Garda?

Con un pullmann della Compagnia Autostradale, che parte da Piazza Castello di fronte al Castello Sforzesco, nel centro della città. Oppure con il treno dalla Stazione Centrale.

Poiché siete così bene informati, saprete anche a quale fermata scendere.

Ci sono tre stazioni per il lago: Desenzano, la più importante, poi Peschiera e Legnago. I treni proseguono per Verona e Venezia, alcuni anche per Trieste.

Garibaldi Terminal and it is expensive, 1500 lire.

Let's go on. Once in Milan, how do you get to Lake Garda?

By the Autostradale Company's coach leaving from Piazza Castello, opposite the Sforza Castle in town, or by train from the Central Station.

Since you know all that, you certainly know also at what station to get off.

There are three stations on the lake: Desenzano, the main one, Peschiera and Legnago. Trains go all the way to Verona and Venice, and some of them to Trieste.

# APPENDIX

1. **Buono, bello, grande** become **buon, bel, gran** before nouns beginning with a consonant:

| | |
|---|---|
| un bel giorno | il gran caldo |
| un buon letto | la gran paura |

Since these are very common adjectives, it is as though the last syllable had been worn out in rapid everyday speech and writing. (Similarly, the Christian name **Giovanni** becomes **Gian** when compounded with a second name, as in **Giancarlo, Gianluca**).

Notice that **grande** is preferred to **gran** in more formal language: **un grande giardino**, etc.

2. **Parecchio, parecchia** are obviously the singular of **parecchi, parecchie** (§81). Used as adjectives, they mean 'a lot of'; as an adverb, **parecchio** means 'a lot'.

| | |
|---|---|
| Voleva comprare parecchia roba. | He wanted to buy a lot of stuff. |
| Abbiamo preso parecchio freddo. | We are chilled to the bone. |
| Ruggero legge parecchio. | Roger reads a good deal. |

3. **Alcuno, alcuna**, singular of **alcuni** (§81) have the same meaning as **nessuno/a** (any) and are used in negative sentences:

| | |
|---|---|
| Tuo figlio non aveva alcuna ragione di comportarsi in quel modo. | Your son had no reason to behave like that. |
| Veramente non c'era alcun bisogno di portare le vostre lenzuola. | There was really no need to bring your sheets. |

4. **Chiunque** (*whoever*), **dovunque** (*wherever*) and **qualunque** (§81) normally demand the subjunctive:

| | |
|---|---|
| Dovunque egli andasse c'era qualcuno che desiderava parlargli. | Wherever he went there was somebody who wanted to speak to him. |
| Qualunque cosa tu faccia ora, non potremo dimenticare chi sei. | Whatever you do now, we cannot forget who you are. |

| | |
|---|---|
| Chiunque avesse notizie del signor XY era pregato di telefonarci. | Whoever knew anything about Mr. XY was asked to phone us. |

**5.** **Ciascuno** is an indefinite pronoun very similar to **ognuno**. It is used especially in some distributive expressions:

| | |
|---|---|
| Prendete una carta per ciascuno. | Take one card each. |

**6.** Some nouns do not take any plural number, among these are foreign words which have long been adopted into Italian, i.e.

| | |
|---|---|
| la crisi, le crisi | la specie, le specie |
| un film, i film | un bar, due bar |

**7.** There are in Italian, as in English, many compound nouns. Those formed with a verb do not take the plural number; the others do, but in various ways, as shown in the lists below:

| | |
|---|---|
| il, i parapiglia | turmoil |
| lo, gli schiaccianoci | nutcracker |
| il, i contachilometri | speedometer |
| la, le portaerei | aircraft carrier |

| | |
|---|---|
| il sottopassaggio | i sottopassaggi, subways |
| il pescespada | i pescispada, swordfish |
| il pettirosso | i pettirossi, redbreasts |
| il passaporto | i passaporti, passports |
| la cassaforte | le casseforti, safes |

**8.** Words like **popolo**, *people*, **governo**, *government*, **assemblea**, *assembly*, **esercito**, *army*, etc., although they indicate several or even a lot of persons, are always used as singular nouns:

il popolo ha sopportato molti sacrifici;
il governo è diviso;
un esercito anche piccolo costa molto allo stato.

Here is a list of common collective nouns that are singular in form but not in meaning:

96

| | |
|---|---|
| legna | firewood |
| roba | stuff; property |
| clientela | customers |
| merce | goods |
| dogana | customs |
| polizía | police |

**9.** The apostrophe and other contractions are used in the following circumstances:

(a) An apostrophe is often substituted for the final vowel of many Italian words (chiefly monosyllables), if the next word begins with a vowel, and especially if the two vowels are identical. This contraction is often—though not always—optional:

| | |
|---|---|
| He helps me. | **(Egli) mi aiuta** *or* **m'aiuta.** |
| Where is the station? | **Dov'è** (*or* **dove è**) **la stazione?** |

(b) When **l**, **m**, **n** or **r** precedes the final vowel, and the next word in the phrase begins with any vowel *or* with any consonant except **z** or an impure **s**, this final vowel can be omitted:

| | |
|---|---|
| Which is his room? | **Qual è** (*or* **quale è**) **la sua stanza?** |
| To sell hats | **Vender cappelli.** |

*but:*

| | |
|---|---|
| To sell shoes | **Vendere scarpe.** |

(c) If a *doubled* consonant precedes the final vowel, one of these consonants is omitted, if (but only if) the final vowel is omitted.

When a final vowel preceded by **l**, **m**, **n** or **r** is dropped, *no apostrophe* is substituted, whether a vowel or a consonant follows. The technical name for this kind of contraction in Italian is **troncamento** (shortening). The substitution of an apostrophe for a final vowel is called **elisione** (elision).

The **troncamento** and the **elisione** are both largely a matter of euphony and custom, rather than of exact rule. You are advised to use them sparingly.

Final vowels omitted from the *plural* form of words (except verbs) are replaced by an apostrophe. That is to say, such a contraction is an **elisione**, not a **troncamento**. An apostrophe is also used if a final **-a** is omitted, except in adverbs:

| | |
|---|---|
| **Nessun'altra** *or* **nessuna altra.** | No other (woman). |

*but:*

| | |
|---|---|
| **Or ora** (NOT **or'ora**). | Just now. |

Two words are sometimes joined together when the last syllable of the first one is stressed. The initial consonant of the second word is then doubled:

|  | piuttosto (=più tosto) | sooner, rather |
|---|---|---|
|  | suddetto (=su detto) | above-mentioned |
|  | davvero (=da vero) | indeed |
|  | sebbene (=se bene) | although |
|  | sì signore *or* sissignore | yes, sir |
| *but* | questa sera *or* stasera | this evening. |

**10.** Verbs ending in **-ciare, -giare** and **-sciare** keep this infinitive sound throughout the conjugation. The -i- is not written before -i or -e:

> **io commercerei** (not **commercierei**)
> **tu commerci** (not **commercii**)

Similarly, verbs ending in **-gliare** and **-gliere** will not retain their -i- before another -i- belonging to the ending:

> **tu scegli** (not **sceglii**)

Finally, notice **tu studi** and **tu odii** (from **studiare, odiare**): the difference results from the necessity to distinguish between these and **tu odi** (from **udire**).

# ITALIAN
# IN THREE MONTHS

# II

## IDIOMS & READING TEXTS

## VOCABULARIES

# INTRODUCTION

Having worked through the grammar lessons in Part I and mastered the basic constructions of the language, the reader will be looking for help with the everyday colloquial expressions that are so necessary for a working grasp of conversational Italian. Obviously it is impossible to include an exhaustive collection of Italian idioms: there is space here to give only some of the most common and most useful. Our point of reference has therefore been the verb. We have chosen the most often-used verbs and listed examples of the expressions and idioms derived from them. The reader should try to foresee what he might want to say in a given situation and build up a vocabulary of phrase and sentence using these examples as a basis.

Following the idioms there is a handful of extracts from some well-known Italian writers. One of the great satisfactions of learning a foreign language is that a new literature becomes available. You should get into the habit of reading Italian as soon as possible: and there is no reason for not starting with the best. We hope these extracts will show you something—a very small something—of what Italian literature has to offer. The English translations on the opposite page should be referred to as little as possible, and we suggest you try reading the Italian pieces aloud.

# IDIOMS

## DARE

| | |
|---|---|
| dare un esame | *to pass an exam* |
| dar battaglia | *to start a battle* |
| darsi delle arie | *to boast about something* |
| darsi da fare | *to get on with something* |
| dare carta bianca | *to grant complete freedom of action* |
| darla a bere; dare ad intendere | *to make someone believe something untrue* |
| darsela a gambe | *to fly* |
| dare frutto | *to yield* |
| dare noia | *to disturb* |

## PRENDERE

| | |
|---|---|
| prendere il toro per le corna | *to deal with determination in difficult circumstances* |
| prendere in giro, per il naso | *to make a fool of someone* |
| o prendere o lasciare | *to take it or leave it* |
| prenderle | *to get beaten (generally, without viciousness)* |
| prendere un granchio | *to make a big mistake* |
| prendere qualcuno con le mani nel sacco | *to catch someone doing something illegal* |
| prendere lucciole per lanterne | *to mistake something for something else (lit. : glow-worms for lamps)* |
| prendere il lutto | *to wear mourning* |
| prendere la mano a qualcuno | *to run out of hand* |
| prender posto | *to sit down* |
| prendersela | *to be offended, to be sorry for something* |

# FARE

| | |
|---|---|
| far festa | to celebrate |
| far la festa a uno (far fuori uno) | to kill someone; to get rid of someone |
| far figura, far colpo | to impress, to be striking |
| fare attenzione | to pay attention |
| fare il callo | to become accustomed to something unpleasant |
| far l'occhio, far l'orecchio, far la mano a qualcosa | to become physically adjusted to something |
| farsi la barba | to shave |
| far fuoco | to fire |
| far le carte | to deal (in card games) |
| far rotta, far vela | to sail |
| far scalo | to call (in a port or airport) |
| fare la fame | to endure hunger, to live in poverty |
| farla a uno | to deceive or damage somebody |

# ESSERE

| | |
|---|---|
| essere di turno | to be on duty, on shift |
| essere di guardia, di cucina, etc. | to be on watch duty, kitchen duty etc. |
| essere di rigore | to be prescribed (of dress) |
| ci siamo! | now! (when the important moment, event or point has come) |
| siamo alle solite! | here we go again (on the recurring of something unpleasant) |
| può essere . . . | it is possible |
| come se nulla fosse | easily |
| essere di parola | to keep one's word |
| essere per qualcuno, per qualcosa | to be favourable to someone, to something |

# AVERE

| | |
|---|---|
| avere colpa di qualcosa | *to be one's fault* |
| aver luogo | *to take place* |
| aver valore | *to be worth* |
| avere a cuore una cosa | *to mean a lot to someone* |
| avere in animo | *to intend* |
| avere in odio | *to hate* |
| avere in simpatia | *to be fond of* |
| avere la luna | *to be in a mood* |
| avere un diavolo per capello | *to be very upset and irritable (lit. : to have as many devils as hairs on one's head)* |
| averne fin sopra i capelli | *to be fed up with something* |
| avercela con uno | *to feel hostile towards somebody* |
| aver voglia di una cosa | *to feel like something* |
| averne da vendere | *to have plenty of something* |

# DIRE

| | |
|---|---|
| dir di sì | *to agree* |
| dir di no | *to refuse* |
| si dice . . . | *they say . . .* |
| non vuol dir nulla | *it doesn't matter* |
| . . . da non dirsi | *. . . beyond words* |
| non c'è che dire | *there is no doubt about it* |
| è tutto dire | *there is no need to add anything* |
| voler dire la sua (opinione) | *to have to say something* |
| dire pane al pane | *to speak sincerely, openly* |

# ANDARE

| | |
|---|---|
| andare giù | *to go down (also figuratively : down the hill)* |
| andare per i fatti propri | *to do one's own business* |
| andare a spasso | *to go for a walk* |
| andare di persona | *to go personally* |

104

| | |
|---|---|
| andare a fondo | *to sink* |
| andare a fondo di una cosa | *to explore all the details of a matter* |
| andare per terra, a gambe per aria | *to fall, to go head over heels* |
| andare coi piedi di piombo | *to act with great caution* |
| andare a tempo (music) | *to keep in time, in step* |
| andare a gonfie vele | *to do very well* |
| andare a vuoto | *to fail, miss* |
| andare a rotoli | *to be ruined, to collapse* |
| andare in rovina | *to go to rack and ruin* |
| andare in malora | *to turn bad, rotten* |
| andare a ruba | *to sell like hot cakes* |
| andare all'aria, a monte | *to fall through* |
| andare per le lunghe | *to take a long time* |
| andare d'amore e d'accordo | *to see eye to eye* |
| andare in fumo | *to come to nothing* |
| andare fuori strada | *to run off, go astray* |
| andare per la maggiore | *to be recognised* |
| non mi va giù | *I can't stand it* |

## STARE

| | |
|---|---|
| stare per (dire) | *to be going to (say)* |
| stare attento | *to pay attention; to mind something* |
| stare zitto | *to be quiet* |
| stare fermo | *to keep still* |
| stare in piedi | *to stand* |
| stare bene, male | *to feel good, unwell; to suit (of clothes or arrangements)* |
| stare di casa | *to live* |
| non ci sta (nella scatola) | *it does not go (into the box)* |

## BEATRICE E VIRGILIO

52    Io era tra color che son sospesi,[1]
      e donna[2] mi chiamò beata e bella,
54    tal che di comandare io la richiesi.
      Lucevan li occhi suoi più che la stella;
      e cominciommi a dir soave e piana,
57    con angelica voce, in sua favella:
      'O anima cortese mantovana,[3]
      di cui la fama ancor nel mondo dura,
60    e durerà quanto il mondo lontana,
      l'amico mio, e non de la ventura,
      ne la diserta piaggia[4] è impedito
63    sì nel cammin, che volt'è per paura;
      e temo che non sia già sì smarrito,
      ch'io mi sia tardi al soccorso levata,
66    per quel ch'i' ho di lui nel cielo udito.
      Or movi, e con la tua parola ornata
      e con ciò ch'ha mestieri al suo campare,
69    l'aiuta sì ch'i' ne sia consolata.
      I' son Beatrice che ti faccio andare;
      vegno del loco ove tornar disío;
72    amor mi mosse, che mi fa parlare.

DANTE ALIGHIERI (1265–1321),
*Inferno*, Canto II

---

1. In Limbus.
2. Beatrice.
3. Virgil was born in Andes, in the neighbourhood of Mantua.
4. Symbol of sinful life.

# BEATRICE AND VIRGIL

52   While I was with the spirits who dwell suspense,
     A Lady summoned me—so blest, so rare,
     I begged her to command my diligence.

55   Her eyes outshone the firmament by far
     As she began, in her own gracious tongue,
     Gentle and low, as tongues of angels are:

58   'O courteous Mantuan soul, whose skill in song
     Keeps green on earth a fame that shall not end
     While motion rolls the turning spheres along!

61   A friend of mine, who is not Fortune's friend,
     Is hard beset upon the shadowy coast;
     Terrors and snares his fearful steps attend,

64   Driving him back; yes, and I fear almost
     I have risen too late to help—for I was told
     Such news of him in heaven—he's too far lost.

67   But thou—go thou! Lift up thy voice of gold;
     Try every needful means to find and reach
     And free him, that my heart rest consoled.

70   Beatrice am I, who thy good speed beseech;
     Love that first moved me from the blissful place
     Whither I'd fain return, now moves my speech.

Trans. DOROTHY SAYERS,
Penguin Books, 1974

## Da LA LOCANDIERA (I, 15)

MIRANDOLINA. Con permissione di V. S.[1] Illustrissima (*finge di voler partire*).

CAVALIERE.[2] ~~Avete premura di partire?~~

MIRANDOLINA. Non vorrei essere importuna.

CAVALIERE. No, mi fate piacere: mi divertite.

MIRANDOLINA. Vede, signore? Così fo[3] con gli altri. Mi trattengo qualche momento; sono piuttosto allegra, dico delle barzellette per divertirli, ed essi subito credono . . . Se la m'intende, e'[4] mi fanno i cascamorti.

CAVALIERE. Questo accade perché avete buona maniera.

MIRANDOLINA (*con una riverenza*). Troppa bontà, illustrissimo.

CAVALIERE. Ed essi s'innamorano!

MIRANDOLINA. Guardi che debolezza! Innamorarsi subito di una donna!

CAVALIERE. Questa io non l'ho mai potuta capire.

MIRANDOLINA. Bella fortezza! Bella virilità!

CAVALIERE. Debolezze! Miserie umane!

MIRANDOLINA. Questo è il vero pensare degli uomini. Signor Cavaliere, mi porga la mano.

CAVALIERE. Perché volete ch'io vi porga la mano?

MIRANDOLINA. Favorisca. Si degni; osservi, sono pulita.

CAVALIERE. Ecco la mano.

MIRANDOLINA. Questa è la prima volta che ho l'onore d'aver per la mano un uomo che pensa veramente da uomo.

CAVALIERE. Via, basta così (*ritira la mano*).

MIRANDOLINA. Ecco. Se io avessi preso per la mano uno di que' due signori sguaiati, avrebbe tosto creduto ch'io spasimassi per lui. Sarebbe andato in deliquio. Non darei loro una semplice libertà, per tutto l'oro del mondo. Non sanno

---

1. Abbreviations of Vostra Signoria. Notice that the Landlady uses the more respectful lei form with the Cavaliere while he uses the voi form with her.

2. Knight. The translator, though, preferred to change it into 'Captain'.

3. A contracted form of 'faccio' (cfr. vo/vado), still used nowadays in Tuscany.

4. Stands for 'essi'.

# From THE LANDLADY (Act I, Sc. 15)

MIRANDOLINA. With your leave, sir.

*Is going.*

CAPTAIN. You are in a hurry.

MIRANDOLINA. I don't want to be troublesome.

CAPTAIN. Not at all; you amuse me.

MIRANDOLINA. You see now for yourself, sir, that is the way I go on with others . . . I keep them in chat for a few minutes. I joke a little to entertain them . . . and then all of a minute— you understand me, sir?—they begin to make love to me.

CAPTAIN. That happens because you have a taking manner.

MIRANDOLINA, *with a curtsy.* You are too kind, sir.

CAPTAIN. And then they lose their hearts.

MIRANDOLINA. What folly to be in such a hurry to lose their hearts!

CAPTAIN. It is a thing I never could understand.

MIRANDOLINA. Talk of strength, indeed! Fine strong men they are.

CAPTAIN. Their weakness is a disgrace to humanity—

MIRANDOLINA. That is right talk for a man. . . . I would like, sir, to shake you by the hand.

CAPTAIN. Why do you want to shake hands with me?

MIRANDOLINA. If you would condescend, sir. See . . . mine is clean.

CAPTAIN. Here is my hand.

MIRANDOLINA. This is the first time I ever had the honour to touch the hand of a man who had the real mind of a man. . . .

CAPTAIN. That will do.

MIRANDOLINA. Look now, if I had held out my hand to either one of that featherbrained pair downstairs, he would have been full sure I was dying for him. He would have lost his heart then and there! I would not have taken any such liberty with them for all the gold in the world. They have no understand-

vivere. Oh benedetto il conversare alla libera! senza attacchi,[5] senza malizia, senza tante ridicole sciocecherie.[6] Illustrissimo, perdoni la mia impertinenza. Dove posso servirla, mi comandi con autorità, e avrò per lei quell'attenzione, che non ho mai avuto per alcuna persona di questo mondo.

CAVALIERE. Per qual motivo avete tanta parzialità per me?

MIRANDOLINA. Perché, oltre il suo merito, oltre la sua condizione, sono almeno sicura che con lei posso trattare con libertà, senza sospetto che voglia far cattivo uso delle mie attenzioni e che mi tenga in qualità di serva senza tormentarmi con pretensioni ridicole, con caricature affettate.

CAVALIERE. Orsù, se avete da badare alle cose vostre, non restate per me.

MIRANDOLINA. Sì signore, vado ad attendere alle faccende di casa. Questi sono i miei amori, i miei passatempi. Se comanderà qualche cosa, manderò il cameriere.

CAVALIERE. Bene . . . Se qualche volta verrete anche voi, vi vedrò volentieri.

MIRANDOLINA. Io veramente non vado mai nelle camere dei forestieri, ma da lei ci verrò qualche volta.

CAVALIERE. Da me . . . perché?

MIRANDOLINA. Perché, illustrissimo signore, ella mi piace assaissimo.

CARLO GOLDONI (1707–1793)

---

5. Literally 'without aggression'.
6. 'Without ridiculous fatuity'.

ing; oh, it's a blessing to be able to say things out without raising suspicion of doing mischief! I beg your pardon, sir, for my forwardness. Whenever I can serve you, just give the order, and I will pay more attention to it than I have ever done for anyone in the whole world.

CAPTAIN. Why should you think so well of me?

MIRANDOLINA. Because you being a well-reared gentleman, I know I can say out my mind to you and have no fear you will think I have an object, or that you will torment me with follies and absurdities.

CAPTAIN. Now, if you want to attend to your business, don't let me keep you here.

MIRANDOLINA. Yes, sir, I will go and look after the housework. That is my delight and my joy. In case you should want anything I will send the servingman.

CAPTAIN. All right. But you might look in at some other time.

MIRANDOLINA. I am not in the habit of attending on my guests . . . but it will be different with you.

CAPTAIN. Why so?

MIRANDOLINA. Because, sir, I like you.

Transl. LADY A. GREGORY in *The Classic Theatre*, Vol. I, Anchor Books, New York, 1958.

# L'ULTIMO INCONTRO DI RENZO E
## DON RODRIGO

Dopo pochi passi, il frate si fermò vicino all'apertura d'una capanna, fissò gli occhi in viso a Renzo, con un misto di gravità e di tenerezza; e lo condusse dentro.

La prima cosa che si vedeva, nell'entrare, era un infermo seduto sulla paglia nel fondo; un infermo però non aggravato, e che anzi poteva parer vicino alla convalescenza; il quale, visto il padre, tentennò la testa, come accennando di no: il padre abbassò la sua, con un atto di tristezza e di rassegnazione. Renzo intanto, girando, con una curiosità inquieta, lo sguardo sugli altri oggetti, vide tre o quattro infermi, ne distinse uno da una parte sur una materassa, involtato in un lenzolo, con una cappa signorile indosso, a guisa di coperta: lo fissò, riconobbe don Rodrigo, e fece un passo indietro; ma il frate, facendogli di nuovo sentir fortemente la mano con cui lo teneva, lo tirò appiè del covile, e, stesavi sopra l'altra mano, accennava col dito l'uomo che vi giaceva.

Stava l'infelice, immoto; spalancati gli occhi, ma senza sguardo; pallido il viso e sparso di macchie nere; nere ed enfiate le labbra: l'avreste detto il viso d'un cadavere, se una contrazione violenta non avesse reso testimonio d'una vita tenace. Il petto si sollevava di quando in quando, con un respiro affannoso; la destra, fuor della cappa, lo premeva vicino al cuore, con uno stringere adunco delle dita, livide tutte, e sulla punta nere.

'Tu vedi!' disse il frate, con voce bassa e grave. 'Può esser gastigo,[1] può esser misericordia. Il sentimento che tu proverai ora per quest'uomo che t'ha offeso, sí; lo stesso sentimento, il Dio, che tu pure hai offeso, avrà per te in quel giorno.[2] Benedicilo, e sei benedetto. Da quattro giorni è qui come tu lo vedi, senza dar segno di sentimento. Forse il Signore è pronto a concedergli un'ora di ravvedimento; ma voleva esserne pregato da te: forse vuole che tu ne lo preghi con quella innocente;[3] forse serba la grazia alla tua sola preghiera, alla preghiera d'un cuore afflitto e rassegnato. Forse la salvezza di quest'uomo e la tua dipende ora

---

1. A less usual form for 'castigo'.
2. The day of judgement.
3. Lucia, the young man's betrothed.

# THE LAST ENCOUNTER
## OF RENZO AND DON RODRIGO

The first thing the young man saw as he went in was a sick man sitting on the straw that covered the ground. He was not desperately ill, however, and looked as if he might soon be convalescent. When he saw Father Cristoforo, he made a little sign, as if to say that there had been no change. The friar bowed his head in sorrowful resignation.

Renzo looked round the room with uneasy curiosity. He noticed three or four invalids, and especially one who was lying a little to one side on a mattress, with a sheet around him and a rich cape on top of it to serve as a blanket. He looked again carefully, saw that it was Don Rodrigo, and started back. But Father Cristoforo tightened the grasp of his left hand on Renzo's wrist, and drew him to the foot of that wretched bed. He stretched out his other hand over it, and pointed with one finger towards the figure that lay there.

The unhappy man was stretched out motionless. His eyes were wide open, but unseeing, his face pale and covered with dark blotches. His lips were black and swollen. It might have been the face of a corpse, except for a violent contraction of the feature which bore witness to a tenacious will to live. His chest heaved from time to time in a painful struggle for breath. His hand lay outside the cape, pressed against the region of his heart with a claw-like grasp of the bloodless fingers, which were black at the tips.

'You see!' said the friar, in low, solemn tones. 'Who knows whether it is a punishment or a mercy? But the feeling that you now have in your heart for this man who has wronged you is the very feeling that God (whom you have wronged) will have for you in his heart on the last day. If you bless this man, you too will be blessed.

'He has been here for four days in the state you see him now, without a sign of consciousness. Perhaps God is ready to grant him an hour in which he can make his peace, but awaits a prayer from you, Renzo. Perhaps a prayer from you and that poor innocent girl, perhaps a prayer from you alone, in the affliction and resignation of your heart. Perhaps this man's salvation—and

113

da te, da un tuo sentimento di perdono, di compassione ...
d'amore!'

Tacque; e, giunte le mani, chinò il viso sopra di esse, e pregò:
Renzo fece lo stesso.

Erano da pochi momenti in quella positura, quando scoccò
la campana. Si mossero tutt'e due, come di concerto; e uscirono.
Né l'uno fece domande, né l'altro proteste: i loro visi parlavano.

ALESSANDRO MANZONI (1785–1873),
da *I Promessi Sposi*, cap. XXXV

## SONO UNA CREATURA

Come questa pietra
del S. Michele[1]
così fredda
così dura
così prosciugata
così refrattaria
così totalmente
disanimata

Come questa pietra
è il mio pianto
che non si vede

La morte
si sconta
vivendo

GIUSEPPE UNGARETTI (1888–1966)
da *Vita di un uomo,* Milano 1958

1. In the Oriental Alps (Carso), where fighting was particularly long
and strenuous in the First World War.

114

your own—depend on you at this moment—on an impulse of forgiveness and pity from you . . . yes—an impulse of love!'

He said no more, but put his hands together, bowed his head, and began to pray. Renzo followed his example.

They had been in that position for a few moments when the chapel bell tolled again. As if at a pre-arranged signal, they both started up and went out together. Father Cristoforo asked no questions and Renzo made no protestations; their faces spoke for their hearts.

Transl. B. PENMAN,
Penguin Classics, 1972.

## I AM A CREATURE

Like this rock
of San Michele
so cold
so hard
so desiccated
so impervious
so utterly
unspirited

Like this rock
are my tears
you cannot see

Death
we redeem
by living

Transl. L. NELSON, JR.,
Contemporary Italian Poetry,
University of California Press, 1962

# I GIOCÀTTOLI ROTTI

L'uomo tarchiato non si era accorto che proprio di faccia a lui, davanti alla porta della latrina, una donna si lamentava sommessamente. Stava seduta su un sacco gonfio, il solito sacco che riappare a certe latitudini come riappare l'asino, e si lamentava. Egli capì che quella donna diceva nel suo dialetto: 'Dov'è andato? Dove se n'è andato?' Era vestita della solita veste nera che copre le madri del popolo da quelle parti, la veste nera che delinea il ventre gonfio, tutta in avanti con l'atteggiamento che si prende sotto quella veste, quello delle mani giunte sul grembo. Poiché si lamentava smarrita nel suo dialetto, ma senza agitarsi, già rassegnata a qualunque evento, l'uomo tarchiato le disse burbero: 'Non vi preoccupate. Sarà salito in qualche altro vagone mentre il treno si muoveva.'

Ella non capì certamente, ma gli credette, si rassegnò. Intuiva soltanto che c'era una spiegazione. E allora si rimise a sedere sul suo sacco, e cominciò a provare un altro giocàttolo, che raffigurava un omino di legno, sempre Fortunello,[1] il quale comandato da una cordicella picchiava con le mani di legno su un ceppo di legno, con un rumore puerile, come forse i pupazzi del presepe odono battere l'incudine del fabbro pastorello di presepe come loro, in una notte soave di Natale in cui gli atti della fatica umana diventano un gioco. Era intenta a questo lavoro quando il figlio riapparve. Ella smise il suo gioco ostinato in cui non capiva, come un gatto non capisce qualcosa che lo incuriosisce e di cui diffida, per dirgli: 'Dove eri andato?' con una voce lontana di vecchio lamento. E l'uomo tarchiato la guardava, curvo su di lei come sul suo stesso passato. Con l'aria di fare un rimprovero a suo figlio, ella gli mostrò il giocàttolo rotto. Il figlio lo osservò. Irrimediabile. Aprì il sacco e lo cacciò dentro. La rassicurò con la voce imperiosa con cui si rassicura una cavalla, e riprese il suo giro inquieto pel corridoio affollato, fra le proteste della folla.

CORRADO ALVARO (1895–1956),
da *Novelle Italiane*, 1962,
Bantam Dual-Language Books

---

1. Fortunello is the Italian version of the comic-strip tramp Happy Hooligan. He became famous through the strips of a children's magazine.

# THE BROKEN TOYS

The stocky man had not noticed that directly facing him, in front of the toilet door, a woman was lamenting in a low voice. She was seated on a full-packed sack—the usual sack which re-appears at certain latitudes just as the donkey reappears—and she was lamenting. He understood that that woman was saying in her dialect: 'Where has he gone? Where has he gone to?' She was dressed in the usual black dress which covers the mothers of the common people in those regions, the black dress which out-lines the swollen belly, all protruded with the posture that they take under that dress, that of the hands joined on the lap. Since she was lamenting, bewildered, in her dialect, but without getting excited, already resigned to any outcome, the stocky man said to her brusquely: 'Don't worry. He must have gotten into some other car while the train was moving.'

She certainly did not understand, but she believed him and resigned herself. She only perceived intuitively that there was an explanation. And then she sat back down again on her sack, and began to try out another toy, which represented a little man of wood, still Happy Hooligan, who, governed by a string, struck with his wooden hands on a wooden block, with a childish noise, such as perhaps the puppets of the Christmas manger hear beat-ing on the anvil of the smith, a little manger shepherd like them-selves, on a gentle Christmas night in which the acts of human toil become a game. She was intent on this work when her son reappeared. She ceased her obstinate activity in which she did not understand, as a cat does not understand, something which excites one's curiosity and which one distrusts, to say to him: 'Where had you gone?' with a distant voice of old lament. And the stocky man looked at her, bending over her as over his own past. With the air of reproaching her son, she showed him the broken toy. The son observed it. Irremediable. He opened the sack and shoved it inside. He reassured her with the imperious voice in which one reassures a mare, and set off again on his rest-less trip through the crowded corridor, among the protests of the crowd.

# IL SASSOFONO

... Un dopopranzo scendeva Anselmo le antiche scale quando da un lungo corridoio—che aveva sul fianco una fuga di porte— gli arrivò un suono umano, una musica, non di violino né di pianoforte o chitarra, ma di uno strumento della musica moderna, del jazz, gli arrivò l'umana voce del sassofono, quello speciale clarinetto argentato a forma di molle snodo di serpente.

Si avvicinò cautamente a dove proveniva quel suono.

Seduto sull'unica sedia di una stanzetta, le pareti nude, un malato stava soffiando sullo strumento.

Aveva la barba, il volto magro, scarnito negli zigomi. Chissà perché si ricordò Anselmo quel personaggio di Stendhal, il poeta Ferrante Palla che fugge per gli intricati boschi.

Quell'uomo sparuto continuava a trarre suoni dallo strumento. Era come invitasse a un tu per tu, sciogliesse ogni sua confidenza, si confessasse, come dicesse: 'Questa voce tesa, questo lungo acuto, è per far intendere l'ira che ebbi un giorno mentre ero innamorato di una mia ragazza bionda. Ed ora, con questa lenta modulazione, muovendo in piccola onda il sassofono, mi chiedo se ero corrisposto. Adesso sto mimando la civetteria femminile, quanto affascinante!'

Aveva il Meschi, quel malato che soffiava nell'argentato sassofono, dei movimenti con la testa e il tronco che richiamavano i delfini quando si alzano bambine-scamente dalle onde oppure veniva in mente un dolce poeta ebbro.

La barba era riccioluta con dei riflessi di rame. Le membra dovevano essere armoniose, agili.

Quello però che davvero affascinava il dottore in ascolto, lo psichiatra Anselmo, era la lucidità della musica, un vero discorso, un eloquio proveniente dal senno e che per di più toccava il cuore; una musica che arrivava a spiegare le sfumature, il passaggio di sottili sentimenti, una bandiera di seta al sole, un damasco esposto al tramonto.

'Che stia spiegando il suo segreto? La storia della sua anima?' si domandò Anselmo. 'Che ora stia aggiungendo, con piangente eloquenza: "Perché, perché non mi capite?".'

MARIO TOBINO (1910–  ),
da *Per le antiche scale*,
A. Mondadori Editore.

# THE SAXOPHONE

. . . One day after lunch as Anselmo was coming down the ancient staircase,[1] from a long corridor that had on its side a suite of doors a human sound of music reached him, not from a violin or piano or guitar, but from an instrument of modern music, jazz; he heard the human voice of the saxophone, that special silver plated clarinet loosely coiled up like a snake.

He cautiously approached the room the sound was coming from. Sitting on the one chair in the bare-walled narrow room a patient was playing the instrument.

He was bearded and his face was thin with prominent cheek-bones. For some reason Anselmo was reminded of the character in Stendhal, the poet Ferrante Palla who takes flight through the tangled woods.

That emaciated man went on drawing sounds from the instrument. It was as if he were inviting someone to a tête à tête, as though he were telling all his secrets, confessing, saying 'This strained voice, this long high note is to signify the anger I felt one day when I was in love with a blonde girlfriend of mine. And now, with this low modulation, moving the saxophone in small waves, I am wondering if my love was reciprocated. Now I am mimicking feminine coquetry—how fascinating it is!'

This patient, Meschi, who was blowing into the silver saxophone, moved his head and body in ways which recalled dolphins when they lift themselves up in the water childishly, or perhaps one thought of a gentle, slightly intoxicated poet.

His beard was curly with copper lights, his limbs must have been harmonious, agile.

However, what really fascinated the listening doctor, Anselmo the psychiatrist, was the lucidity of the music; it was a veritable discourse which was not only intelligent but touched the heart as well: it was a music that managed to express the nuances and the flow of the subtlest feelings; it was a silken banner in sunlight, a brocade caught by the setting sun.

'Is he telling us his secret—the history of his soul?' wondered Anselmo. 'And is he now saying with tearful eloquence: "Why don't you understand me, why?"?'

---

1. They belonged to a very old monastery which had become a mental hospital.

# VOCABULARIES

## TRAVELLING

**By car ...**

*accelerator*, acceleratore *m.*; *back axle*, ponte posteriore *m*; *battery*, batteria *f*; *bend*, curva *f*; *big end*, testa di biella *f*; *body*, telaio *m*; *bolt*, bullone *m*; *bonnet*, cofano *m*; *boot*, portabagagli *m*; *brake*, freno *m*; *brake* (*v*), frenare; *brake lining*, guarnizioni freni *f*; *break-down*, guasto *m*; *break down* (*v*), subire un gausto; *breakdown van*, autosoccorso *m*; *bulb*, lampadina *f*; *bumper*, paraurto *m*; *camshaft*, albero distribuzione *m*; *can*, recipiente *m*; *car*, autovettura *f*, automobile *m*; *caravan*, roulotte *f*; *carburettor*, carburatore *m*; *clutch*, frizione *f*; *choke*, starter *m*; *distributor*, distributore *m*; *diversion*, deviazione stradale *f*; *door*, porta *f*; *drive*, guidare; *driver*, guidatore *m*; *driving licence*, patente di guida *f*; *dynamo*, dinamo *f*; *engine*, motore *m*; *exhaust*, scappamento *m*; *fan*, ventilatore *m*; *fan belt*, cinghia del ventilatore *f*; *funnel*, imbuto *m*; *garage*, autorimessa *f*; *gear*, rapporto *m*; *gear-box*, cambio *m*; *gear lever*, leva del cambio *f*; *grease*, grasso *m*; *handle*, manovella *f*; *hood*, capote *f*; *horn*, avvisatore acustico *m*; *highway code*, codice della strada *m*; *hub*, mozzo *m*; *ignition*, accensione *f*; *ignition key*, chiave della accensione *f*; *indicator*, indicatore *m*; *inner tube*, camera d'aria *f*; *insurance certificate*, certificato d'assicurazione *m*; *jack*, martinetto *m*; *lights* (*head*), fari *m*; *lights* (*side*), luci di posizione *f*; *lights* (*rear*), luci posteriori *f*; *lorry*, autocarro *m*; *lubrication*, lubrificazione *f*; *luggage rack*, portabagagli *m*; *mechanic*, meccanico *m*; *mirror*, retrovisore *m*; *motorist*, automobilista *m, f*; *motorway*, autostrada *f*; *number plate*, targa *f*; *nut*, dado *m*; *oil*, olio *m*; *one-way*, senso unico *m*; *overheat*, surriscaldare; *park*. parcheggiare; *no parking*, divieto di parcheggio; *pedestrian*, pedone *m*; *petrol*, benzina *f*; *petrol pump*, distributore di benzina *m*; *piston ring*, segmento *m*; *plug*, candela *f*; *propeller shaft*, albero di transmissione *m*; *puncture*, foratura *f*; *radiator*, radiatore *m*; *repair*, riparare; *right of way*, precedenza *f*; *rim*, cerchione *m*; *road*, strada *f*; *road* (*major*) strada di grande communicazione *f*; *road* (*minor*) strada secondaria *f*; *road closed*, strada chiusa al traffico *f*; *run out of petrol*, esaurire la benzina; *screw*, vite *f*; *screwdriver*, cacciavite *m*; *shock absorber*, ammortizzatore, *m*; *skid*, slittare; *spanner*, chiave *f*; *spares*, ricambi *m*; *speed*, velocità *f*; *speed limit*, limite di velocità *m*; *speedometer*, contachilometri; *spring*, molla *f*; *starter*, starter *m*; *steering wheel*, volante *m*; *street*, strada *f*; *tank*, serbatoio *m*; *toll*, pedaggio *m*; *traffic lights*, semaforo *m*; *trailer*, rimorchio *m*; *transmission*, trasmissione *f*; *two-stroke mixture*, miscela *f*; *tyre*, pneumatico *m*; *tyre (spare)* ruota di ricambio *f*; *tyre (tubeless)* gomma tubeless *f*: *tyre pressure*, pressione di gonfiaggio *f*; *underpass*, sottopassaggio *m*; *uneven road*, strada irregolare *f*; *valve*, valvola *f*; *van*, furgoncino *m*; *vehicle*, veicolo *m*; *washer*, rondella *f*; *wheel*, ruota *f*; *wheel, (rear)* ruota posteriore *f*; *wheel (front)*, ruota anteriore *f*; *window*, finestrino *m*; *window (rear)*, lunotto *m*; *windscreen*, parabrezza *m*; *windscreen wiper*, tergicristallo *m*; *wing*, parafango *m*.

## By Train, Boat and Plane . . .

*aeroplane*, aeroplano *m*; *air conditioner*, climatizzatore *m*; *air hostess*, hostess *f*; *airline*, linea aerea *f*; *airport*, aeroporto *m*; *air terminal*, aerostazione *f*; *altitude*, quota *f*; *anchor*, ancora *f*; *arrival*, arrivo *m*; *ashtray*, portacenere *m*; *boat*, nave *f*; *booking office*, ufficio prenotazioni *m*; *bunk*, cuccetta *f*; *bus*, autobus *m*; *cabin*, cabina *f*; *captain*, comandante *m*; *case*, valigia *f*; *change trains*, cambiar treno; *cloudy*, nuvoloso; *coach*, vagone *m*; *compartment*, scompartimento *m*; *connection*, coincidenza *f*; *control tower*, torre di controllo *f*; *corridor*, corridoio *m*; *crew* equipaggio *m*; *crossing*, traversata *f*; *Customs*, Dogana *f*; *Customs duty*, tasse doganali *f*; *Customs officer*, doganiere *m*; *deck*, ponte *m*; *declare*, dichiarare; *delayed*, in ritardo; *departure*, partenza *f*; *destination*, destinazione *f*; *dining car*, vagone ristorante *m*; *disembark*, sbarcare; *door*, porta *f*; *embark*, imbarcare; *emergency exit*, uscita di sicurezza *f*; *engine*, motore *m*; *enquiry office*, ufficio informazioni *m*; *entrance*, ingresso *m*; *escalator*, scala mobile *f*; *exit*, uscita *f*; *fare*, tariffa *f*; *ferry*, traghetto *m*; *flight*, volo *m*; *fog*, nebbia *f*; *foghorn*, sirena *f*; *funnel*, fumaiolo *m*; *get on (a train, etc)* salire su; *get off*, scendere da; *goods train*, treno merci *m*; *guard*, capotreno *m*; *hand luggage*, bagaglio a mano *m*; *heating*, riscaldamento *m*; *jet aircraft*, aviogetto *m*; *jet engine*, motore a getto *m*; *label*, etichetta *f*; *land (v)*, atterrare; *late*, in ritardo; *lavatory*, toeletta *f*; *left-luggage office*, ufficio consegna bagagli *m*; *lifeboat*, scialuppa di salvataggio *f*; *life-jacket*, giubbotto di salvataggio *m*; *lift*, ascensore *m*; *luggage*, bagaglio *m*; *luggage rack*, ripiano bagagli *m*; *luggage van*, bagagliaio *m*; *ocean*, oceano *m*; *passport*, passaporto *m*; *pilot*, pilota *m*; *platform*, piattaforma *f*; *port*, porto *m*; *porter*, facchino *m*; *propeller*, elica *f*; *queue*, coda *f*; *queue* (*v*), fare la coda; *route*, rotta *f*; *runway*, pista *f*; *sea*, mare *m*; *seat*, posto *m*; *seat belt*, cintura di sicurezza *f*; *seat reservation*, prenotazione *f*; *sleeper*, posto nel vagone letto *m*; *sleeping berth*, cuccetta *f*; *speed*, velocità *f*; *station*, stazione *f*; *stationmaster*, capostazione *m*; *steward*, steward *m*; *stop*, fermata *f*; *stop* (*v*), fermarsi; *storm*, temporale *m*; *take-off*, decollo *m*; *taxi*, tassi *m*; *terminus*, stazione di testa *f*; *ticket* (*single*), biglietto d'andata *m*; *ticket* (*return*), biglietto d'andata e ritorno *m*; *ticket inspector*, controllore *m*; *timetable*, orario *m*; *tip*, mancia *f*; *track*, binario *m*; *train*, treno *m*; *train* (*express*), rapido *m*; *travel* (*v*), viaggiare; *tray*, vassoio *m*; *trunk*, baule *m*; *underground*, metropolitana *f*; *waiting room*, sala d'aspetto *f*; *weather report*, bollettino metereologico; *window*, finestrino *m*.

## EATING AND DRINKING

*almond*, mandorla *f*; *anchovy*, acciuga *f*; *aperitif*, aperitivo *m*; *apple*, mela *f*; *apricot*, albicocca *f*; *artichoke* (*globe*), carciofo *m*; (*Jerusalem*) topinamburo *m*; *asparagus*, asparago *m*; *aubergine*, melanzana *f*; *avocado*, avocado *m*; *bacon*, bacon, *m*; *banana*, banana *f*; *basil*, basilico *m*; *batter*, pastetta *f*; *bay leaf*, lauro *m*; *bean*, fagiolo *m*; *beef*, manzo *m*; *beer*, birra *f*; *beetroot*, barbabietola *f*; *biscuit*, biscotto *m*; *blackberry*, mora *f*; *blackcurrant*, ribes *m*; *boar*, cinghiale *m*; *boiled*, lessato *m*; *bone*, osso *m*; *brains*, cervella *f*; *brandy*, cognac *m*; *brazil nut*, mandorla del Brasile *f*; *bread*, pane *m*; *breadcrumbs*, pangrettato *m*; *broth*, brodo *m*; *brussels sprouts*, broccoletti *m*; *butter*, burro *m*; *cabbage*, cavolo *m*; *cake*, focaccia *f*, dolce *m*; *caper*, cappero *m*; *caraway*, cumino *m*; *cheese*, formaggio *m*; *chervil*, cerfoglio *m*; *cherry*, ciliegia *f*; *chicken*, pollo *m*; *chicory*, indivia *f*; *chive*, aglio cipollino *m*; *chocolate*, cioccolato *m*; *chop*, cotoletta *f*; *cider*, sidro *m*; *cinnamon*, cannella *f*; *clam*, mollusco *m*; *clove*, chiodo di garofano *m*; *cockle*, cuore *m*; *cocoa*, cacao *m*; *coconut*, noce di cocco *f*; *cod*, merluzzo *m*; *coffee*, caffé *m*; *coriander*, coriandolo *m*; *cornflour*, farina di granoturco *f*; *crab*, gambero *m*; *cream*, panna *f*; *cucumber*, cetriolo *m*; *damson*, susina *f*; *date*, dattero *m*; *dessert*, dessert *m*; *diet*, regime *m*; *dough*, pasta *f*; *duck*, anatra *f*; *duckling*, anatroccolo *m*; *eel*, anguilla *f*; *egg*, uovo *m*; *eggplant*, melanzana *f*; *escallop* (*of meat*), scaloppina *f*; *fat*, grasso *m*; *fennel*, finocchio *m*; *fig*, fico *m*; *fish*, pesce *m*; *fizzy*, frizzante; *non-fizzy*, non frizzante; *flan*, flan (per torta di frutta) *f*; *flour*, farina *f*; *fruit*, frutta *f*; *game*, cacciagione *f*; *garlic*, aglio *m*; *giblets*, frattaglie *m*; *gherkin*, cetriolino *m*; *gin*, gin *m*; *goose*, oca *f*; *gooseberry*, uva spina, *f*; *grape*, uva *f*; *grapefruit*, pompelmo *m*; *gravy*, sugo *m*; *greengage*, susina Regina Claudia *f*; *green pepper*, peperone *m*; *grilled*, ai ferri; *haddock*, aglefino *m*; *hake*, nasello *m*; *ham*, prosciutto *m*; *hare*, lepre *f*; *heart*, cuore *m*; *herbs*, erbe aromatiche *f*; *herring*, aringa *f*; *ice cream*, gelato *m*; *ice cube*, cubetto di ghiaccio *m*; *icing sugar*, zucchero velato *m*; *jam*, marmellata *f*; *jelly*, gelatina *f*; *kidney*, rognoncino *m*; *lamb*, agnello *m*; *lard*, lardo *m*; *leek*. porro *m*; *lemon*, limone *m*; *lemonade* (*fizzy*), limonata gazzosa; (*still*) limonata *f*; *lemon juice*, succo di limone *m*; *lentil*, lenticchia *f*; *lettuce*, lattuga *f*; *liver*, fegato *m*; *lobster*, aragosta *f*; *lollipop*, caramella *f*; *macaroon*, amaretto *m*; *mackerel*, sgombro *m*; *marmalade*, marmellata d'arance *f*; *marrow*, zucca *f*; *marrow* (*baby*), zucchino *f*; *marzipan*, marzapane *m*; *meat*, carne *f*; *melon*, melone *m*; *meringue*, meringa *f*; *milk*, latte *m*; *minced meat*, carne tritata *f*; *mineral water*, acqua minerale *f*; *mint*, menta *f*; *mushroom*, fungo *m*; *mussel*, cozza *f*; *mustard*, senape *f*; *mutton*, carne di montone *f*; *mutton* (*leg of*), zampa di montone; *nougat*, mandorlato *m*; *nut*, noce *f*; *nutmeg*, noce moscata *f*; *oil*, olio *m*; *olive*, oliva *f*; *omelette*, frittata *f*; *onion*, cipolla *f*; *orange*, arancia *f*; *orangeade*, aranciata *f*; *orange juice*, succo d'arancia *m*; *oyster*, ostrica *f*; *pancake*, frittella *f*; *paprika*, paprica *f*; *parsley*, prezzemolo *m*; *partridge*, pernice *f*; *pasta*, pasta *f*; *pastry*, pasta per pasticceria *f*; *pastries*, pasticceria *f*; *paté*, paté *m*; *pea*, pisello *m*; *peach*, pesca *f*; *peanut*, arachidi *f*; *pear*, pera *f*; *pepper*, pepe *m*; *pheasant*, fagiano *m*; *picnic*, picnic *m*; *pigeon*, piccione *f*; *pineapple*, ananas *m*; *plaice*, pianuzza *f*; *plum*, prugna *f*; *poached*, affogato *m*; *pork*, maiale *m*; *port*, porto *m*; *potato*, patata *f*; *poultry*, pollame *m*; *prawn*, gamberetto *m*; *prune*, prugna *f*; *quail*, quaglia *f*; *rabbit*, coniglio *m*; *radish*, ravanello *m*; *raisin*, uva passa *f*; *raspberry*, lampone *m*; *redcurrant*, ribes *m*; *rhubarb*, rabarbaro *m*; *rice*, riso *m*; *roast*, arrosto *m*; *roe* (*hard*), uova di pesce *f*; *roe* (*soft*), latte di pesce; *roll*, panino *m*; *rosemary*, ramerino *m*; *rum*, rum *m*; *saffron*, zafferano *m*; *sage*, salvia *f*; *salad*, insalata *f*; *salmon*, salmone *m*; *salt*, sale *m*; *sandwich*,

panino imbottito *m*; *sardine*, sardina *f*; *sauce*, salsa *f*; *sausage*
(*cooked*), salcicciotto *m*; *sausage* (*raw*), salciccia *f*; *scallop*, pettine
*m*; *seasoning*, condimento *m*; *semolina*, semola *f*; *shallot*, scalogno
*m*; *sherry*, sherry *m*; *shrimp*, gamberetto *m*; *skate*, razza *f*;
~~*smoked*, affumicato~~; ~~*soda water*, aqua di selz *f*~~; *sole*, sogliola *f*;
*soup*, minestra *f*; *spaghetti*, spaghetti *m*; *spice*, spezie *f*; *spinach*,
spinaci *m*; *starter*, antipasto *m*; *steak*, bistecca *f*; *stew*, stufato
*m*; *stock*, brodo *m*; *strawberry*, fragola *f*; *stuffed*, farcito *m*;
*stuffing*, ripieno *m*; *suet*, grasso di rognone *m*; *sugar*, zucchero *m*;
*sultana*, uva sultana *f*; *sweets*, dolci *m*; *sweetbreads*, animella *f*;
*syrup*, sciroppo *m*; *tangerine*, mandarino *m*; *tarragon*, targone *m*;
*tart*, torta *f*; *tea*, té *m*; *thyme*, timo *m*; *toast*, crostino *m*; *toffee*,
caramella *f*; *tomato*, pomodoro *m*; *tongue*, lingua *f*; *tonic water*,
acqua brillante *f*; *tripe*, trippa *f*; *trout*, trota *f*; *tuna*, tonno *m*;
*turbot*, rombo *m*; *turkey*, tacchino *m*; *turnip*, rapa *f*; *vanilla*,
vaniglia *f*; *veal*, vitello *m*; *vegetable*, legumi *m*; *vinegar*, aceto *m*;
*vitamin*, vitamina *f*; *walnut*, noce *f*; *water*, acqua *f*; *watercress*,
crescione *m*; *whiting*, merlano *m*; *wine*, vino *m*; *winkle*, littorina
*f*; *woodcock*, beccaccia *f*; *yeast*, lievito *m*; *yoghurt*, yogurt *m*.

## HOUSE AND HOUSEHOLD

*address book*, agenda indirizzi *f*; *adhesive tape*, nastro adesivo *m*;
*ant*, formica *f*; *armchair*, poltrona *f*; *ashtray*, portacenere *m*;
*axe*, accetta *f*; *balcony*, balcone *m*; *basket*, paniere *m*; *bath*,
bagno *m*; *bathroom*, sala da bagno *f*; *beam*, trave *f*; *bed*, letto *m*;
*bed* (*double*), letto matrimoniale *m*; *bedroom*, camera da letto *f*;
*bedbug*, cimice *f*; *bee*, ape *f*; *binoculars*, binoccolo *m*; *blanket*,
coperta *f*; *bleach*, varechina *f*; *block of flats*, isolato *m*; *blotting
paper*, carta assorbente *f*; *bluebottle*, moscone *m*; *biro*, penna
biro *f*; *boiler*, caldaia *f*; *bolt*, bullone *m*; *bolt* (*door*), catenaccio
*m*; *book*, libro *m*; *bookcase*, libreria *f*; *bottle*, bottiglia *f*; *bowl*
(*eating*), scodella *f*; *bowl* (*washing*), lavello *m*; *box*, scatola, *f*;
*brick*, mattone *m*; *briefcase*, cartella *f*; *broom*, scopa *f*; *brush*,
spazzola *f*; *bucket*, secchio *m*; *button*, bottone *m*; *camp-bed*,
lettino da campo *m*; *candle*, candela *f*; *candle-stick*, candeliere
*m*; *carpet* (*fitted*), mochette *f*; *carpet* (*loose*), tappeto *m*; *ceiling*,
soffitto *m*; *cellar*, cantina *f*; *central heating*, riscaldamento centrale *m*; *chair*, sedia *f*; *chest*, cassapanca *f*; *chimney*, camino
*m*; *clock*, pendolo *m*; *clothespeg*, molletta *f*; *cloakroom*, guarda-

roba *m*; *coal*, carbone *m*; *coat hanger*, attaccapanni *m*; *comb*, pettine *m*; *cooker*, cucina *f*; *corkscrew*, cavatappi *m*; *cot*, lettino *m*; *cotton*, filo da cucito *m*; *cottonwool*, cotono idrofilo *m*; *cupboard*, credenza *f*; *cushion*, cuscino *m*; *curtain*, tenda *f*; *decanter*, caraffa *f*; *deck chair*, sedia a sdraio *f*; *desk*, scrittoio *m*; *detergent*, detersivo *m*; *dictionary*, dizionario *m*; *dining-room*, sala da pranzo *f*; *dishcloth*, strofinaccio per piatti *m*; *doll*, bambola *f*; *doll's house*, casa da bambola *f*; *door*, porta *f*; *door* (*front*) portone *m*; *door* (*back*), portina *f*; *doorbell*, campanello *n*; *doorknob*, battacchio *m*; *drain*, tubo di scarico *m*; *drainpipe*, tubo di spurgo *m*; *draught*, corrente d'aria *f*; *drawer*, tiretto *m*; *drawing-pin*, puntina da disegno *f*; *dry rot*, putrefazione secca *f*; *dust*, polvere *f*; *dustbin*, pattumiera *f*; *duster*, strofinaccio *m*; *eggcup*, portauovo *m*; *eiderdown*, piumino *m*; *elastic*, elastico *m*; *electricity*, elettricità *f*; *envelope*, busta *f*; *file* (*for documents*), archivio *m*; *file* (*tool*), lima *f*; *filter*, filtro *m*; *fire*, fuoco *m*; *fireplace*, caminetto *m*; *flannel*, flanella *f*; *flat*, appartamento *m*; *flea*, pulce *f*; *floor*, pavimento *m*; *flower pot*, vaso per fiori *m*; *fly*, mosca *m*; *fork*, forchetta *f*; *fountain pen*, penna stilografica *f*; *fridge*, frigorifero *m*; *frying pan*, padella *f*; *funnel*, imbuto *m*; *furnished*, ammobiliato *m*; *fuse*, fusibile *m*; *garden*, giardino *m*; *gas*, gas *m*; *gas cylinder*, bombola *f*; *gas meter*, contatore *m*; *glass*, bicchiere *m*; *greenhouse*, serra *f*; *ground sheet*, tappeto a terra *m*; *gutter*, grondaia *f*; *glue*, colla *f*; *hairbrush*, spazzola per capelli *f*; *hall*, entrata *f*; *hammer*, martello *m*; *handbag*, borsa *m*; *high chair*, seggiolone *m*; *hinge*, cerniera *f*; *hoe*, zappa *f*; *hook*, gancio *m*; *hook and eye*, uncino con maglietta *m*; *hot water bottle*, borsa termica *f*; *ink*, inchiostro *m*; *insulation*, isolamento *m*; *iron*, ferro da stiro *m*; *iron* (*v*), stirare; *ironing board*, asse per stirare *m*; *jamb*, stipite *m*; *jug*, brocca *f*; *kettle*, bollité *m*; *key*, chiave *f*; *keyhole*, buco della serratura *m*; *kitchen*, cucina *f*; *knife*, coltello *m*; *knit*, lavorare a maglia; *knitting needle*, ferro da maglia *m*; *ladder*, scala *f*; *ladle*, mestolo *m*; *lamp* (*bedside*), lampada da letto *f*; *lampshade*, paralume *m*; *laundry*, bucato *f*; *lavatory*, toeletta *f*; *lavatory paper*, carta igienica *f*; *lawn*, prato *m*; *lawnmower*, tosatrice per prati *f*; *letterbox*, buca delle lettere *f*; *light*, luce *f*; *light switch*, interruttore *m*; *lighter*, accendisigaro *m*; *lighter flint*, pietrina focaia *f*; *lighter fuel*, bomboletta per accendisigaro *f*; *lightning conductor*, parafulmine *m*; *lock*, serratura *f*; *magazine*, periodico *m*; *map*, cartina *f*; *mat*, stuoino *m*;

*matches*, fiammiferi *m*; *mattress*, materasso *m*; *methylated spirit*, alcool denaturato *m*; *mirror*, specchio *m*; *mosquito*, zanzara *f*; *mouse*, topo *m*; *nail*, chiodo *m*; *nail* (*finger-*), unghia *f*; *nailbrush*, spazzolino per unghie *m*; *nailfile*, limetta *f*; *napkin*, tovagliolo *m*; *nappy*, pannolino *m*; *needle*, ago *m*; *nib*, pennino *m*; *nut*, dado *m*; *oil can*, oliatore *m*; *oven*, forno *m*; *paint*, vernice *f*; *paper*, carta *f*; *paper clip*, serracarte *m*; *paper tissues*, fazzoletti di carta *m*; *paraffin*, petrolio *m*; *pencil*, matita *f*; *penknife*, coltellino *m*; *photograph*, fotografia *f*; *piano*, pianoforte *m*; *picture*, quadro *m*; *pillow*, cuscino *m*; *pillowcase*, federa *f*; *pin*, spillo *m*; *plate*, piatto *m*; *pliers*, pinze *f*; *plug*, spina *f*; *polish*, cera a lucidare *f*; *popper*, bottone a molla *m*; *pram*, carrozzino per bambini *m*; *primus stove*, fornello a petrolio *m*; *pushchair*, passeggino *m*; *radiator*, radiatore *m*; *rake*, rastrello *m*; *rates*, imposte municipale *f*; *razor*, rasoio *m*; *razor blade*, lametta *f*; *razor* (*elecrtic*), rasoio elettrico *m*; *record*, disco *m*; *record player*, giradischi *m*; *rent*, pigione *f*; *roof*, tetto *m*; *room*, camera *f*; *rope*, corda *f*; *rubber*, gomma *f*; *rubbish*, immondizia *f*; *rucksack*, zaino *m*; *safety pin*, spilla di sicurezza *f*; *satchel*, cartella *f*; *saucepan*, casseruola *f*; *saucer*, sottocoppa *f*; *saw*, sega *f*; *scales* (*bathroom*), bilancia da bagno *f*; *scissors*, forbici *f*; *screw*, vite *f*; *screwdriver*, cacciavite *f*; *scrubbing brush*, spazzola rigida *f*; *sewing machine*, macchina per cucire *f*; *shampoo*, shampoo *m*; *shaving brush*, pennello *m*; *shaving soap*, sapone per barba *m*; *shears*, cesoie *f*; *shoe brush*, spazzola per scarpe *f*; *shower*, doccia *f*; *shutter*, imposte *f*; *sink*, lavello *m*; *sitting room*, salotto *m*; *soap*, sapone *m*; *sofa*, divano *m*; *spanner*, chiave *f*; *spoon*, cucchiaio *m*; *stairs*, scala *f*; *stamp* (*postage*), francobollo *m*; *stool*, sgabello *m*; *strap*, cinghia *f*; *string*, spago *m*; *suitcase*, valigia *f*; *sun tan cream*, crema per abbronzatura *f*; *table*, tavola *f*; *tablecloth*, tovaglia *f*; *talc*, talco *m*; *tap*, rubinetto *m*; *tape measure*, metro a nastro *m*; *tape recorder*, registratore *m*; *teapot*, teiera *f*; *telephone*, telefono *m*; *telephone directory*, guida telefonica *f*; *telephone number*, numero telefonico *m*; *telephone operator*, centralinista *m*, *f*; *television*, televisore *m*; *thermos*, termos *m*; *thermostat*, termostato *m*; *thimble*, ditale *m*; *tile*, tegola *f*; *tin opener*, apriscatole *m*; *toothbrush*, spazzolino per denti *m*; *toothpaste*, dentifricio *f*; *torch*, lampada tascabile *f*; *towel*, asciugamano *m*; *tray*, cassoio *m*; *trunk*, baule *m*; *tweezers*, pinzette *f*; *typewriter*, macchina da scrivere *f*; *umbrella*. ombrello *m*; *unfurnished*, non ammobiliato; *vacuum cleaner*, aspirapolvere *m*; *vase*, vaso *m*; *voltage*, tensione *f*; *walking stick*, canna *f*; *wall*, parete *f*; *wallet*, portafogli *m*; *wardrobe*, guardaroba *m*; *washbasin*, lavabo *m*; *washer*, rondella *f*; *washing line*, corda per stendere *f*; *washing machine*, lavabiancheria *f*; *wasp*, vespa *f*; *waste paper basket*, cestino della cartaccia *m*; *water-colour*, acquarello *m*; *water heater*, riscaldatore per acqua *m*; *waterproof*, impermeabile; *wheelbarrow*, carriola *f*; *wire*, filo metallico *m*; *wireless*, radio *f*; *wool*, lana *f*; *writing paper*, carta da lettere *f*.

## SHOPS AND SERVICES

*antique dealer*, antiquario *m*; *art gallery*, galleria d'arte *f*; *baker*, panetteria *f*; *book shop*, libreria *f*; *builder*, costruttore *m*; *butcher*, macelleria *f*; *café*, caffé *m*; *cake shop*, pasticceria *f*; *carpenter*, falegname *m*; *chemist*, farmacia *f*; *cinema*, cinema *m*; *cleaners*, tintoria *f*; *comedy*, commedia *f*; *confectioner*, pasticceria *f*; *dairy*, latteria *f*; *decorator/painter*, decoratore *m*; *department store*, grande magazzino *m*; *do the shopping*, fare la spesa; *draper*, negoziante di stoffe *m*; *dustmen*, spazzaturaio *m*; *electrician*, elettricista *m*; *estate agent*, agente immobiliare *m*; *film*, film *m*; *fireman*, vigile del fuoco *m*; *fishmonger*, pescivendolo *m*; *fruiterer*, fruttivendolo *m*; *gas company*, società del gas *f*; *garage*, autorimessa *f*; *grocer*, droghiere *m*; *hairdresser*, parrucchiere per signora *m*; *hire a car*, noleggiare una vettura; *ironmonger*, negoziante di ferramenta *m*; *jeweller*, gioielleria *m*; *library*, biblioteca *f*; *market*, mercato *m*; *museum*, museo *m*; *newsagent*, giornalaio *m*; *office*, ufficio *m*; *perfumery*, profumeria *f*; *play*, rappresentazione *f*; *plumber*, idraulico *m*; *police station*, commissariato *m*; *policeman*, poliziotto *m*; *postman*, postino *m*; *post office*, ufficio postale *m*; *restaurant*, ristorante *m*; *retailer*, dettagliante *m*; *shoe repairer*, calzolaio *m*; *shoe shop*, calzoleria *f*; *snackbar*, snakbar *m*; *stationer*, cartolaio *m*; *supermarket*, supermercato *m*; *swimming pool*, piscina *f*; *tailor*, sarto *m*; *theatre*, teatro *m*; *tobacconist*, tabaccaio *m*; *travel agency*, agenzia turistica *f*; *wholesaler*, grossista *m*; *window cleaner*, lavafinestra *m*; *wine merchant*, commerciante in vini *m*; *zoo*, giardino zoologico *m*.

## CLOTHES, ETC.

*anorak*, giacca a vento *f*; *apron*, grembiule *m*; *bathing costume*, costume da bagno *m*; *belt*, cintura *f*; *beret*, berretto *m*; *bikini*, bikini *m*; *blouse*, camicetta *f*; *boots*, stivali *m*; *bow tie*, farfallino *m*; *bracelet*, bracialetto *m*; *braces*, bretelle *f*; *brassiere*, reggiseno *m*; *brooch*, spilla *f*; *buckle*, fibbia *f*; *buttonhole*, asola *f*; *cap*, berretto *m*; *cape*, cappa *f*; *clothing*, indumenti *m*; *coat*, cappotto *m*; *collar*, colletto *m*; *collar stud*, bottone per colletto *m*; *corset*, busto *m*; *cotton*, cotone *m*; *cuff*, polsino *m*; *cufflinks*, gemelli *m*; *curlers*, bigodini *m*; *darn*, rammendare, *dress*, vestito *m*; *dress* (*v*) vestirsi; *dress-suit*, abito da cerimonia *m*; *dressing-gown*, vestaglia *f*; *dry-clean*, pulire a secco; *earrings*, orecchini *m*; *embroider*, ricamare; *embroidery*, ricamo *m*; *engagement ring*, anello di fidanzamento *m*; *eye pencil*, matita per sopracciglia *f*; *face-powder*, cipria *f*; *fringe*, frangetta *f*; *glove*, guanto *m*; *hair-clip*, molletta per capelli *f*; *hair-net*, reticella *f*; *hairpin*, forcina *f*; *hat*, cappello *m*; *handkerchief*, fazzoletto *m*; *jacket*, giubba *f*; *jeans*. jeans *m*; *knickers*, mutande *f*; *lace*, pizzo *m*; *lapel*, risvolto *m*; *lawn*, batista *f*; *leather*, cuoio *n*; *lipstick*, rossetto *m*; *make-up*, trucco *m*; *nail-varnish*, lacca *f*; *necklace*, collana *f*; *nightdress*, camicia da notte *f*; *nylon*, nylon *m*; *overall*, tuta (grembiule), *mf*; *overcoat*, soprabito *m*; *pants*, calzoni *m*; *petticoat*, sottoveste *f*; *pocket*, tasca *f*; *pony-tail*, coda di cavallo *f*; *powder-compact*, portacipria *m*; *pyjamas*, pigiama *m*; *raincoat*, impermeabile *m*; *ribbon*, nastro *m*; *ring*, anello *m*; *rollers*, bigodini *m*; *sandals*, sandali *m*; *satin*, raso *m*; *scarf*, sciarpa *f*; *sew*, cucire; *shawl*, scialle *m*; *shirt*, camicia *f*; *shoes*, scarpe *f*; *shoe-laces*, lacci per scarpe *m*; *silk*, seta *f*; *size*, misura *f*; *skirt*, gonna *f*; *sleeve*, manica *f*; *slippers*, pantofole *f*; *socks*, calzini *m*; *starch*, amido *m*; *stockings*, calze *f*; *suit* (*man's*), abito *m*; *suit* (*woman's*), completo *m*; *sun glasses*, occhiali da sole *m*; *T-shirt*, camicetta *f*; *tennis shoes*, scarpe da tennis *f*; *tie*, cravatta *f*; *tights*, calze-maglia *f*; *trousers*, pantaloni *m*; *undress*, spogliarsi; *uniform*, uniforme *f*; *veil*, velo *m*; *velvet*, velluto *m*; *waistcoat*, panciotto *m*; *wedding ring*, fede *f*; *wellington boots*, stivaloni *m*; *wig*, parrucca *f*; *zip fastener*, chiusura lampo *f*.

## BODY

*adam's apple*, pomo d'Adamo *m*; *ankle*, caviglia *f*; *arm*, braccio *m*; *artery*, arteria *f*; *back*, schiena *f*; *beard*, barba *f*; *bladder*, vescica *f*; *blood*, sangue *m*; *body*, corpo *m*; *bone*, osso *m*; *brain*, cervello *m*; *breast*, seno *m*; *buttock*, natica *f*; *cheek*, guancia *f*; *chest*, torace *m*; *chin*, mento *m*; *ear*, orecchio *m*; *eardrum*, timpano *m*, *ear lobe*, lobo *m*; *elbow*, gomito *m*; *eye*, occhio *m*;

*eyeball*, bulbo oculare *m*; *eyebrow*, sopracciglio *m*; *eyelash*, ciglio *m*; *face*, viso *m*; *fist*, pugno *m*; *forehead*, fronte *f*; *gall bladder*, cistifellea *f*; *gland*, ghiandola *f*; *gums*, genvive *f*; *hair*, capelli *m*; *hand*, mano *f*; *head*, capo, *m*; *heart*, cuore *m*; *hip*, anca *f*; *intestine*, intestino *m*; *joint*, articolazione *f*; *knee*, ginocchio *m*; *kneecap*, rotula *f*; *kidney*, rene *m*; *leg*, gamba *f*; *lip*, labbro *m*; *liver*, fegato *m*; *lung*, polmone *m*; *mouth*, bocca *f*; *muscle*, muscolo *m*; *nail*, unghia *m*; *navel*, ombelico *m*; *neck*, collo *m*; *nipple*, cappezzolo *m*; *nose*, naso *m*; *nostril*, narice *f*; *organ*, organo *m*; *palate*, palato *m*; *palm*, palmo *m*; *pancreas*, pancreas *m*; *parting*, scriminatura *m*; *shoulder*, spalla *f*; *skin*, epidermide *f*; *skull*, cranio *m*; *spleen*, milza *f*; *stomach*, stomaco *m*; *teeth*, denti *m*; *thigh*, coscia *f*; *throat*, gola *f*; *thumb*, pollice *m*; *toes*, dita del piede *f*; *tongue*, lingua *f*; *tonsil*, tonsilla *f*; *vein*, vena *f*; *wrist*, polso *m*.

## MEDICAL

*abortion*, aborto *m*; *abscess*, ascesso *m*; *accident*, incidente *m*; *acne*, acne *f*; *allergic*, allergico; *allergy*, allergia *f*; *anaesthetic*, anestesia *f*; *antibiotic*, antibiotico *m*; *antibody*, anticorpo *m*; *antidote*, antidoto *m*; *antiseptic*, antisettico *m*; *appendicitis*, appendicite *f*; *arthritis*, artrite *f*; *aspirin*, aspirina *f*; *athlete's foot*, tigna *f*; *backache*, mal di schiena *m*; *bacteria*, batteri *m*; *bandage* (*v*), bendare; *bandage*, benda *f*; *bandage* (*crêpe*) fascia *f*; *birth*, nascita *f*; *blackhead*, acne *f*; *bleed*, sanguinare; *blister*, vescica *f*; *blood*, sangue *m*; *blood group*, gruppo sanguigno *m*; *boil*, foruncolo *m*; *broken*, spezzato; *bronchitis*, bronchite *f*; *bruise*, contusione *f*; *bump*, gonfiore *m*; *burn*, ustione *f*; *cancer*, cancro *m*; *casualty ward*, astanteria *f*; *catarrh*, catarro *m*; *cerebral haemorrhage*, emorragia cerebrale *f*; *chicken pox*, varicella *f*; *choke*, suffocare; *clot*, grumo *m*; *cold*, raffreddore *m*; *concussion*, commozione cerebrale *m*; *constipation*, stitichezza *f*; *consultant*, consulente *m*; *convalescence*, convalescenza *f*; *corn.* callo *m*; *cough* (*v*), tossire; *cough*, tosse *f*; *cough mixture*, sciroppo contro la tosse *m*; *cramp*, crampo *m*; *cut*, taglio *m*; *cyst*, ciste *f*; *dandruff*, forfora *f*; *dentist*, dentista *m*; *diabetes*, diabete *m*; *diarrhoea*, diarrea *f*; *disinfectant*, disifettante *m*; *doctor*, medico *m*; *dose*, dose *f*; *drug*, sostanze medicinali *f*; *earache*, mal d'orecchi *m*; *emetic*, emetico *m*; *enema*, enteroclisma *m*; *epidemic*, epidemia *f*; *epilepsy*, epilessia *f*; *faint*, svenire; *false teeth*, denti artificiali *m*; *fever*, febbre *f*; *filling* (*dental*), otturazione *f*; *flat feet*, piedi piatti *m*; *'flu*, influenza *f*; *fracture*, frattura *f*; *gallstone*, calcolo biliare *m*; *gargle*, gargarizzare; *germ*, microbo *m*; *German measles*, rosolia *f*; *graft*, trapianto *m*; *graze*, abrasione *f*; ~~haemorrhage, emorragia *f*; hay fever, febbre da fieno *f*;~~ *headache*, emicrania *f*; *heart attack*, crisi cardiaca *f*; *hernia*, ernia *f*; *hospital*, ospedale *m*; *ill*, ammalato; *illness*, malattia *f*; *injection*, iniezione *f*; *injured*, ferito; *inoculation*, inoculazione *f*; *insect bite*, puntura d'insetto *f*; *insomnia*, insonnia *f*; *iodine*, iodio *m*; *laxative*, lassativo *m*; *laryngitis*, laringite *f*; *measles*, morbillo *m*; *medicine*, medicamento *m*; *menstrual period*, mestruazioni *f*; *miscarriage*, aborto *m*; *mole*, neo *m*; *mumps*, orecchioni *m*; *nervous breakdown*, collasso nervoso *m*; *nose bleed*, epistassi *f*; *nurse*, infermiera *f*; *ointment*, unguento *m*; *operating theatre*, sala operatoria *f*; *operation*, intervento chirurgico *m*; *pain*, dolore *m*; *patient*, paziente *m*; *piles*, emorroidi *f*; *pill*, pillola *f*; *pleurisy*, pleurite *f*; *pneumonia*, polmonite *f*; *poison*, veleno *m*; *poultice*, cataplasma *m*; *pregnancy*, gravidanza *f*; *pregnant*, incinta; *prescription*, ricetta *f*; *rash*, eruzione *f*; *Red Cross*, la Croce Rossa *f*; *rheumatism*, reumatismo *m*; *sanitary towels*, assorbente igienico *m*; *scratch*, graffio *m*; *sea sickness*, mal di mare *m*; *sedative*, calmante *m*; *shivering*, tremito *m*; *sighted* (*short*), miope; (*long*), presbite; *sinus*, sinusite *f*; *sleeping pill*, sonnifero *m*; *sling*, benda *f*; *slipped disc*, ernia del disco *f*; *smallpox*, vaiolo *m*; *sore throat* infiammazione alla gola *f*; *spectacles*, occhiali *m*; *splint*, stecca *f*; *splinter*, spina *f*; *spot*, chiazza (pustola) *f*; *sprain*, lussazione *f*; *stiff neck*, torcicollo *m*; *sting*, puntura *f*; *stitch* (*surgical*), sutura *f*; *stomach ache*, mal di stomaco *m*; *stomach upset*, dolore allo stomaco *m*; *stretcher*, lettiga *f*; *stroke*, attacco *m*; *stye*, orzaiolo *m*; *sunburn*, scottatura *f*; *sunstroke*, insolazione *f*; *surgeon*, chirurgo *m*; *surgery*, ambulatorio *m*; *swelling*, rigonfiamento *m*; *tablet*, compressa *f*; *tapeworm*, tenia *m*; *temperature*, temperatura *f*; *thermometer*, termometro *m*; *therapy*, terapia *f*; *tonsillitis*, tonsillite *f*; *toothache*, mal di denti *m*; *truss*, cinto erniario *m*; *tuberculosis*, tubercolosi *f*; *tumor* tumore *m*; *ulcer*, ulcera *f*; *unconscious*, inconscio; *varicose vein*, vene varicose *f*; *verruca*, verruca *f*; *virus*, virus *m*; *visiting hours*, orario di visita *m*; *vomit* (*v*), vomitare; *water on the knee*, sinovite *f*; *ward*, corsia *f*; *wart*, porro *m*; *whooping cough*, pertosse *f*; *X-ray*, radiografia *f*; *yellow jaundice*, itterizia *f*.

# ITALIAN IN THREE MONTHS

## III

### KEY TO GRAMMAR EXERCISES

## Key to Lesson 1

EXERCISE I. 1 un allievo; 2 una persona; 3 una stazione; 4 un arrivo; 5 uno scoppio; 6 una strada; 7 un posto; 8 un'altalena; 9 uno stecco; 10 un'erba.

EXERCISE II. 1 arrivi; 2 due strade; 3 un cartello; 4 posti; 5 due stazioni; 6 un posto; 7 dieci minuti; 8 un minuto; 9 un caffè, due caffè; 10 un tè.

EXERCISE III. 1 I have; 2 I have not; 2 they have not; 4 have you?; 5 they have; 6 have you not?; 7 you have not; 8 tu hai, voi avete; 9 essi non hanno; 10 abbiamo? 11 non abbiamo? 12 ha.

## Key to Lesson 2

EXERCISE 1. 1 il padre, i padri; 2 una sorella, le sorelle; 3 la madre, le madri; 4 un fratello, i fratelli; 5 l'appartamento, gli appartamenti; 6 lo spazio, gli spazi; 7 le scale; 8 un acróbata, gli acróbati; 9 lo záino, gli záini; 10 l'inglese, gl'inglesi.

EXERCISE II. 1 lei è la sorella; 2 (essi) sono gli invitati; 3 tu sei Franco?; 4 siamo fratello e sorella; 5 sono in ritardo?; 6 voi siete studenti.

EXERCISE III. 1 caffè per due, per piacere; 2 sulla sedia; 3 la porta dell'appartamento; 4 al tempo dei Romani; 5 Anna è in cucina; 6 sulla strada.

## Key to Lesson 3

EXERCISE I. 1 nostra madre; 2 i vostri parenti; 3 il loro arrivo; 4 i nostri programmi; 5 vostro zio è giovane, la loro zia è giovane; 6 a uno a uno; 7 o l'uno o l'altro; 8 i loro caffè.

EXERCISE II. 1 la pagina nuova; 2 un fiore giallo; 3 venti freddi; 4 le giovani insegnanti; 5 il nostro viaggio è corto; 6 le vostre sedie sono strette; 7 le stelle sono lucenti; 8 un forte colpo; 9 due sorelle grasse; 10 un libro spesso.

EXERCISE III. 1 troviamo che . . .; 2 ascolti molto; 3 parlate bene; 4 se invito i Martelli; 5 accéttano; 6 il tempo passa in fretta; 7 ascoltiamo insieme; 8 accetti.

## Key to Lesson 4

EXERCISE I. 1 le mie lettere; 2 il tuo giornale; 3 i suoi zii; 4 i tuoi libri e il mio; 5 il loro appartamento e il vostro (tuo); 6 vostra figlia e le mie nipoti; 7 io compro le mie cartoline, lui compra le sue; 8 quale sedia è più comoda, la tua o la sua?; 9 qui ábita un suo amico; 10 a volte incontro due tuoi allievi.

EXERCISE II. 1 è molto ammalato?; 2 abbiamo tempo per comprare un giornale?; 3 hai una foto di Gianni?; 4 quando arrivano i tuoi genitori?; 5 andate in vacanza insieme?; 6 è pronta la cena?

EXERCISE III.   1 no, signora, Lei ha torto;   2 Lei è il signor Brilli?;
3 Lei e la sua famiglia vívono in Inghilterra?;   4 arriva sempre tardi;
5 sono in vacanza;   6 Lei lavora troppo.   ᗆ ᒋ.

## Key to Lesson 5

EXERCISE I.   1 non credo;   2 credete?;   3 credo che …;   4 i bambini crédono a Babbo Natale;   5 Anna crede tutto (ogni cosa);   6 credi
a me …

EXERCISE II.   1 scrivo lentamente in italiano;   2 Anna e Carlo
mandano regolarmente delle cartoline;   3 aspetta tranquillamente di
cominciare;   4 il negozio del villaggio è straordinariamente ben fornito;
5 normalmente la biblioteca è aperta.

EXERCISE III.   1 c'è una núvola in ciela;   2 ci sono delle barche in
mare;   3 c'è una difficolta;   4 Ci sono delle fragole in giardino?;   5 ci
sono regali e regali;   6 c'è tempo;   7 c'è una sorpresa per voi;   8 ci sono
due signori nel suo ufficio.

## Key to Lesson 6

EXERCISE I.   1 dórmono;   2 agíscono;   3 serviamo;   4 capiamo;
5 capisci?;   6 non capisce;   7 dorme;   8 segue;   9 capisco;   10 non
seguo.

EXERCISE II.   1 ha mandato dodici rose;   2 hanno trovato mille lire;
3 ho temuto il peggio;   4 non ha i creduto;   5 siamo arrivati;   6 avete
capito?;   7 sono andati?;   8 è partita;   9 è stato il primo;   10 sei
stato/a gentile.

EXERCISE III.   1 abbiamo trovato un fiore raro; lo conoscete?;   2 no,
non l'abbiamo mai visto prima;   3 abbiamo studiato queste materie;   4 io
le ho dimenticate;   5 le hanno domandate;   6 dove sei stato?;   7 ti ho
cercato dappertutto;   8 mi spiace, signore, il direttore non la può ricevere
oggi, ma la riceverà domani alle úndici.

## Key to Lesson 7

EXERCISE I.   1 abiterete insieme?;   2 porteranno abbastanza
gelato?;   3 sarai pronta alle tre, Teresa?;   4 certo, sono io che ti aspet-
terò;   5 avrai molto lavoro?;   6 sì, ma sarà interessante;   7 ci
racconterai?;   8 vi dirà tutto mia moglie;   9 visiteremo prima Roma,
poi Bologna;   10 torneremo per l'ora di cena.

EXERCISE II.   1 quante persone hai invitato?;   2 dimmi quale vestito
devo mettere;   3 che cosa cercate?;   4 chi gioca con la signorina
Ross?;   5 qual è la mia camera?;   6 chi ha preso la chiave del laboratorio
è pregato di rimetterla a posto;   7 che hai fatto?;   8 il signor Martelli
desidera sapere quanto vi deve.

EXERCISE III.   1 pochi giorni;   2 le banche;   3 gli antichi Greci;
4 sono cárichi di pacchi;   5 archeólogi tedeschi;   6 nelle botteghe.

## Key to Lesson 8

EXERCISE I. 1 ascoltate!; 2 aspetta; 3 finite la bottiglia; 4 spegnete la luce; 5 accendete; 6 dormi.

EXERCISE II. 1 corri; correte; 2 non aver paura, non abbiate paura; 3 non aprire la porta, non aprite la porta; 4 va' piano, andate piano; 5 non essere curioso, non siate curiosi; 5 sii puntuale, siate puntuali; 7 abbi fede, abbiate fede; 8 non aver fretta, non abbiate fretta.

EXERCISE III. 1 ti risponderò subito; 2 vi ripete le sue parole; 3 le portano delle caramelle; 4 gli parlerete, allora?; 5 la torre dicontrollo dà loro la posizione; 6 questo libro mi è dedicato.

## Key to Lesson 9

EXERCISE I. 1 il secondo volume è più importante del primo; 2 nei paesi ci sono meno abitanti; 3 il ristorante francese è più simpatico; 4 è anche più caro; 5 chi ha il numero più alto?; 6 vince la carta più bassa.

EXERCISE II. 1 ecco Pietro, di cui hai già conosciuto i genitori; 2 il giovane che hai accompagnato alla stazione è molto simpatico; 3 il signore che ci farà la conferenza sarà presto qui; 4 avevano una figlia che amavano teneramente; 5 vedo bambini che giocano, genitori che bevono la birra; 6 le persone con cui Sara lavora sono tedesche.

EXERCISE III. 1 andate in macchina o in aereo?; 2 il contadino va al mercato; 3 mia madre fa così; 4 le sigarette fanno male; 5 mi dai quel piatto?; 6 quanto ti danno per il lavoro che hai fatto?; 7 non siete stati attenti; 8 noi stiamo sempre attenti; 9 fa' come ti ho detto; 10 andate e tornate presto; 11 da' a Cesare quello che è di Cesare; 12 hai dato l'acqua alle piante?

## Key to Lesson 10

EXERCISE I. 1 Pietro ha ricevuto tre regali, forse domani ne avrà un altro; 2 la barca di Giovanni è stupenda, anche noi ne avremo una così; 3 sono andati a Génova una volta e ci vanno di nuovo quest' anno; 4 il terremoto, chi ci ha mai pensato?

EXERCISE II. 1 questa volta abbiamo guadagnato poco; 2 prendete quello che vi serve; 3 non capisco quella donna; 4 se volete visitare i giardini, chiedete a quest'uomo; 5 guarda i dáini vicino al fiume!; 6 quegli animali sono diventati rari; 7 quello sciocco di Pietro ne ha ucciso uno; 8 questa me la pagherà!

EXERCISE III. 1 mi impresteresti il vocabolario russo?; 2 che ne direste di uscire per un'ora?; 3 Mario sarebbe contento di vedervi; 4 direi di sì; 5 la coppia del quarto piano avrebbe una stanza da affittare; 6 volete vederla?

# Key to Lesson 11

EXERCISE I.  1 andavano bene quelle lettere?;  2 sì, grazie, le ho già spedite;  3 il cattivo umore dello straniero durava due o tre giorni, poi passava ed egli parlava di nuovo con tutti;  4 mentre la sorella chiudeva la valigia, Alberto telefonò per avere un tassì;  5 il lunedì sera giocavano a carte, il venerdì giocavano al bigliardo in un bar.

EXERCISE II.  1 questa è una buona stoffa e costa di più;  2 quell'uomo intelligente e coraggioso troverà una soluzione;  3 la tua vecchia zia l'ha combinata bella;  4 oggi ci sono brutte notizie;  5 il barómetro dice: variábile;  6 questo mare calmo e cielo azzurro dureranno circa tre giorni;  7 il viaggio è stato orribile ma corto, per fortuna.

EXERCISE III.  1 il disegno dell'architetto non è piaciuto al conte;  2 ai gatti non piace l'acqua;  3 gli piacerebbe fare un viaggio, e a te?;  4 questa è la Sua camera; spero che Le piacerà;  5 il maggiordomo dice che al tuo amico piácciono i mobili antichi.

EXERCISE IV.  1 puoi fare quello che vuoi, può fare quello che vuole, possiamo fare quello che vogliamo, possono fare quello che vogliono;  2 sono, sei, è libero, siamo, sono liberi fino alle 4,15;  3 voglio, vuoi, vogliamo, volete, vogliono partire alle 4,30 in punto;  4 devo, devi, deve, dobbiamo, dovete tornare al torpedone in tempo.

# Key to Lesson 12

EXERCISE I.  1 mi dispiace, il tuo libro non mi interessa, e te lo rendo;  2 la padrona di casa ha del buon vino: se glielo chiedete, ve ne darà;  3 ve lo dicevo, che oggi sarebbe tornato il bel tempo!;  4 poiché i fatti sono accertati, li racconterò loro.

EXERCISE II.  1 passando all'economia della regione, osserviamo che . . .;  2 adoprando questo prodotto otterrete ottimi risultati;  3 mio cognato fa un affare, comprando quella casa;  4 avendo ricevuto le informazioni necessarie sull'incidente, possiamo scrivere il rapporto. 5 essendo povera di ferro e di carbone, l'Italia deve importarli.

EXERCISE III.  1 Il signor Rondi sta telefonando;  2 i ragazzi stanno studiando, verranno più tardi;  3 il battello sta arrivando;  4 stavamo parlando della gita.

EXERCISE IV.  1 la palla ce l'ha Renato, préndigliela!;  2 réndimeli; ti prego di réndermeli;  3 andiámocene;  4 váttene;  5 tu hai tante riviste, dáccene qualcuna;  6 stavo parlándoglene;  7 rispondendo loro;  8 Teresa ha scritto di mandarle una foto;  9 mandiámoglela; 10 sentivano i padroni litigare furiosamente.

# Key to Lesson 13

EXERCISE I.  1 che io porti, portiamo, portiate, portino; che io portassi, portasse, portássimo, portaste, portassero;  2 venda, vendiamo, vendiate, véndano; vendessi, vendesse, vendéssimo, vendeste, vendéssero;  3 agisca, agiamo, agiate, agiscano; agissi, agisse, agissimo, agiste, agissero.

Exercise II.   1 non è giusto che lascino a me tutti i lavori noiosi; 2 sarebbe meglio che facéessimo insieme quel rapporto;   3 il direttore pensa che lei sia la persona piú adatta per trattare con il sig. Brambilla; 4 speriamo che le merci siano arrivate in buono stato;   5 mia moglie desiderava che la casa fosse pronta prima delle vacanze;   6 spero che stiate tutti bene e che veniate presto a trovarci.

Exercise III.   1 bisogna domandare a loro;   2 loro non ti diranno niente;   3 le occorre qualcosa, dottore?   4 bisogna che telefoni súbito a mio fratello Giorgio;   6 perché proprio a lui?;   6 se vi occorrono dei portatori indigeni, dítelo a me;   7 i genitori lasciarono al figlio l'appartamento grande e tennero per sé quello piccolo.

## Key to Lesson 14

Exercise I.   1 mi sveglio sempre presto;   2 a che ora ti alzi?;   3 Anna si sta lavando;   4 ci pettiniamo di nuovo prima di pranzo; 5 vestítevi e andate via di qui;   6 le indossatrici si cambiano in fretta; 7 Roberto era l'ultimo a coricarsi;   8 ci scusiamo per l'errore.

Exercise II.   1 Bianca si è dimenticata di comprare le sigarette; 2 se fuma sempre così, si ammalerà;   3 sedétevi e raccontate dal principio;   4 l'alpinista si arrampicava con facilità sulla roccia;   5 se non vi sforzate di giocare meglio, è inutile continuare l'allenamento; 6 non preoccuparti, i danni della pioggia non sono gravi.

Exercise III.   1 hanno fatto loro alcuni dolci, gli altri li hanno comprati;   2 Luigi ha qualcosa da dirti, Giovanna;   3 il vecchio ha lasciato tutto a qualcuno che conosceva appena;   4 date una scodella di riso a ognuno;   5 il lavoro è facile, chiunque lo imparerebbe;   6 darei qualunque cosa per essere lasciato in pace;   7 nessuno sapeva niente; 8 alcuni soldati fuggirono altri invece caddero prigionieri.

## Key to Lesson 15

Exercise I.   1 furono anni duri per la giovane coppia;   2 la loro prima figlia non andò a scuola fino all'età di dieci anni;   3 la madre, che era muestra, le insegnò a leggere e a scrivere;   4 quando il vino nuovo fu pronto, venne un negoziante e lo comprò tutto;   5 a noi rimase solo la quantità necessaria per il consumo famigliare;   6 il presidente della nostra società sedette accanto alla moglie del sindaco.

Exercise II.   1 in questa regione i terreni si comprano a poco prezzo; 2 il parco fu venduto;   3 al suo posto si vedono ora numerose villette; 4 promettiamo che saranno costruiti un nuovò ospedale e la biblioteca; 5 gli abitanti del villaggio sono stati ingannati;   6 la promessa non fu mantenuta.

Exercise III.   1 la strada che sale al Gran San Bernardo è larga e comoda;   2 io sono già uscita, perché non esci un po' tu?   3 dopo la tempesta viene il sereno;   4 Bruno e Teresa erano divenuti i suoi migliori amici;   5 cose simili avvengono per ragioni precise;   6 il quadro che ammirate proviene dalla Villa Fóscari;   7 la nonna è salita in camera a riposare;   8 i tulipani non sono venuti bene.

## Key to Lesson 16

Exercise I. 1 sapévano, séppero;  2 dovevi, dovesti;  3 voleva, volle; starai; saprete; potranno;  7 potrébbero;  8 uscirai;  9 uscireste; 10 verremo;  11 verremmo; vorremmo;  13 andate;  14 andrete; 15 esci;  16 vieni.

Exercise II. 1 se andassi io?;  2 se veníssero loro?;  3 è meglio che sappiate;  4 era ora che salíssimo;  5 è ora che egli salga;  6 se dovesse dare la chiave, la darebbe;  7 potrebbe tradirvi, se volesse;  8 che lo voglia o no, mio fratello dovrà darmi il denaro;  9 dovendo recarmi nella sua città ho pensato di scriverle.

## Key to Lesson 17

Exercise I. 1 perché dite così?;  2 diciamo queste cose perché sono vere;  3 bevi questa medicina, ti farà bene;  4 il marinaio bevve;  5 che ne diresti di una passeggiata dopo cena?;  6 ho paura che faccia freddo;  7 se fa freddo metteremo una giacca;  8 i superstiti dissero che era stata una ritirata spaventosa;  9 il capitano stava facendo il rapporto.

Exercise II. 1 le condizioni del malato non destano preoccupazioni, è tutto quello che ha detto il dottore;  2 mandateci rifornimenti a sufficienza, è tutto quello che vi chiediamo;  3 chissà se i quattro uomini resisteranno ancora a lungo;  4 chissà quando smetterà di piovere;  5 mi domando se oggi Ruggero prenderà la patente;  6 il giudice voleva sapere se quelle parole erano veramente tutto quello che l'imputato aveva detto la sera del 18.

Exercise III. 1 questa è la piazza in cui aspettano;  2 l'unica sera in cui siamo in casa tutti e due è il venerdì;  3 chissà se mia cognata mi restituirà le 10.000 lire che le ho prestato;  4 per quello che ne sappiamo noi, Vanna è una donna a posto;  5 non appena mi avrà pagato ve lo dirò.

## Key to Lesson 18

Exercise I. 1 chiudiamo le finestre perché non entrino le zanzare;  2 benché esercitasse una professione difficile, Edmondo diventò ricco;  3 il ragazzo era disposto a qualsiasi sacrificio purché gli lasciassero studiare il violino;  4 la città era cresciuta senza che ce ne accorgessimo;  5 se il treno avesse avuto due minuti di ritardo, l'avremmo preso;  6 vi ho fatti venire tutti affinché conosciate mio fratello Pietro, l'americano;  7 la gente dica quello che vuole, io faccio come mi pare.

Exercise II. 1 i cacciatori sono molti, la selvaggina è poca;  2 il giovane era andato solo poche volte al cinema;  3 abbiamo pochi soldi, vorremmo una stanza che non costi molto;  4 con un po' di pazienza il lavoro verrà proprio bene;  5 il vecchio aveva detto poco, ma quel poco permise al giornalista di capire molte cose;  6 eravamo in molti a prendere il traghetto per Messina.

EXERCISE III. 1 ho un amico che conosce tutte le canzoni in voga; 2 una sera sente una canzone nuova e io giorno dopo la sa già tutta; 3 naturalmente sa tutto di ogni cantante e musicista; 4 per lui il maggiore divertimento è di ascoltare le sue orchestrine preferite; 5 i suoi fratelli non lo capiscono; 6 è una cosa normale, non tutti hanno gli stessi gusti.

## Key to Lesson 19

EXERCISE I. 'Mi accade abbastanza spesso di fare questo sogno. Avere davanti agli occhi una pagina scritta, e doverla leggere. Il tormento non incomincia subito. Leggo qualche linea ma a poco a poco incomincia a diventare difficile —— perché sul foglio compaiono non più parole, ma cose. Oggetti: un aratro, una sedia. Eppure io *devo* leggere. Faccio un tremendo sforzo per tradurre in parole le cose, ma mancando i nessi non riesco a combinare un discorso. Cerco si inventare, ma sento sempre più che il senso mi sfugge, mentre tanto più pesano con la loro massiccia evidenza, le cose.'

LALLA ROMANO, de *La villeggiante*, 1975

EXERCISE II. 1 Renzo Ricci era un bravissimo attore, andavo sempre a vederlo; 2 dopo l'operazione era molto debole, debolissimo; 3 i suoi figli andavano spessissimo a trovarlo all'ospedale; 4 si tratta del migliore ospedale della città; 5 ce ne sono tre buonissimi, ma questo è ottimo; 6 la prevenzione delle malattie non ha minore importanza della cura, anzi; 7 la media degli studenti legge solo due libri al mese, al massimo tre; 8 non c'è maggior dolore che ricordarsi del tempo felice nella miseria (Dante).

## Key to Lesson 20

EXERCISE I. alcune scrittrici italiane moderne sono molto interessanti; 2 chi avrebbe mai detto che Adele sarebbe diventata una brava giornalista?; 3 la pediatra dice che Tommasino non può mangiare né dolci né caramelle; 4 una disegnatrice di mode guadagna quello che vuole; 5 nell'antichità vi furono anche delle profetesse, non solo dei profeti.

EXERCISE II. 'And what have you done with your jacket, your trousers, and your cap?'

'I met with robbers who took them from me. Tell me, good old man, could you perhaps give me some clothes to return home in?'

'My boy, as to clothes, I have nothing but a little sack in which I keep lupins. If you want it, take it; there it is.'

Pinocchio did not wait to be told twice. He took the sack at once and, with a pair of scissors he cut a hole at the end and at each side, and put it on like a shirt. And with this slight clothing he set off for the village.

Transl. M. A. MURRAY, London, Dent.

'My mother is a terrible pessimist. She is very distrustful. She would stand in a corner, by the window, watching those small pans of hers, frightened, suspicious, embittered, in her light Japanese housecoat and her thin braid of hair twisted at the top of her head with a piece of black elastic.'

139

# INDEX TO GRAMMAR LESSONS

140

# VOCABULARY INDEX

Included are most words introduced in the earlier exercises. The numbers indicate paragraphs dealing in depth with that particular word.

141

CAKE *dolce*
camp site *campeggio*
can *posso*
cannot *non puo*
cap *berretto*
car *macchina, auto-*
  *mobile*
careful *attento*
cat *gatto*
cathedral *cattedrale*
certainly *certo*
chair *sedia*
channel *canale*
children *bambini*
cigarrette *sigaretta*
city *città*
clothes *vestiti*
cloud *nuvola*
coach *torpedone*
coal *carbone*
coat *giacca*
coffee *caffè*
cold *freddo*
to come *venire* 86
to come back *tornare*
to come from *provenire*
comfortable *comodo*
company *società*
to continue *continuare*
to count *contare*
couple *coppia*
cup *tassa*
to cure *medicare*

DAUGHTER *figlia*
day *giorno*
dealer *negoziante*
dearly *teneramente*
to deceive *ingannare*
deer *daino, -i*
to dedicate *dedicare*
design *disegno*
dictionary *dizionario*
difficulty *difficoltà*
dinner *cena*
to do *fare* 52, 90
doctor *medico*
door *porta*
to get dressed *vestirsi*

drill *trapano*
to drink *bere*
driver *autista*
to drown *annegare*
dumpling *gnocco*

EACH *ogni*
earthquake *terremoto*
easy *facile*
easily *facilmente*
eight *otto*
engineer *tecnico*
Englishman *inglese*
to enjoy oneself
  *divertirsi* 76
enough *abbastanza,*
  *basta*
evening *sera*
everything *tutto*
everywhere *dapper-*
  *tutto*
extraordinary
  *straordinario*

FACT *fatto*
family *famiglia*
famous *famoso*
fantastic *stupendo*
farmer *contadino*
fat *grasso*
father *padre*
few *poco*
to find *trovare*
to finish *finire* 32
first *primo*
five *cinque*
flat (n.) *appartamento*
floor (storey) *piano*
flower *fiore*
to follow *seguire*
for *per*
to forestall *provenire*
to forget *dimenticare*
four *quattro*
Friday *venerdì*
friend *amico*
from *da*
furniture *mobili*

GARDEN *giardino*
gentleman *signore*
girl *ragazza*
to give *dare* 50
glad *contento*
to go *andare* 50
to go out *uscire* 86
to go up *salire* 85
good *buono*
good morning
  *buongiorno*
grass *erba*
ground *terreno*
guest *invitata*

HALL *entrata, sala*
hard *duro*
to happen *avvenire*
to have *avere* 3
to have to *dovere* 62
he *lui, egli* 4
to hear *sentire*
to help oneself
  *servirse* 76
here *ecco*
him, her (dir. obj.)
  *lo, la* 35
his, her *suo, sua* 19
holiday *vacanza*
hospital *ospedale*
how much, many?
  *quanto?*

I *io* 3
icecream *gelato*
idea *idea*
if *se*
ill *ammalato*
illness *malattia*
to import *importare*
in *in*
to interest *interessare*
interesting *interessante*
to investigate *indagare*
to invite *invitare*
iron *ferro*
it *esso* 4
it (dir. obj.) *lo, la* 35
Italian *italiano*
its *suo, sua* 19

142

JOURNEY *viaggio*
to jump *saltare*

TO KEEP *mantenere*
key *chiave*
kind *gentile*
kitchen *cucino*
knapsack *zàino*
knife *coltello*
to know *sapere* 62,
  *conoscere*

LAND *terra*
land (property) *terreni*
landlady *padrona*
late *in retardo*
to leave *partire* 32
to lend *imprestare*
less than *meno . . . di,*
  *meno . . . che*
to let (room) *affittare*
letter *lettera*
library *biblioteca*
lipstick *rossetto*
to live *vivere, abitare*
to look *guardare*
to look for *cercare*
loud *forte*
to love *amare*

MADAM *signora*
magazine *rivista*
to make *fare* 52, 90
man *uomo*
manager *direttore*
match *fiammifero*
market *mercato*
mayor *sindaco*
me (dir. obj.) *mi* 35
to meet *incontrare*
midday *mezzogiorno*
minute *minuto*
mistake *sbaglio*
model (fashion)
  *indossatrice*
Monday *lunedì*
more than *più . . . di,*
  *più . . . che*
mother *madre*
much *molto*

musician *musicista*
my *mio, -e, -èi, -e* 19

NARROW *stretto*
new *nuovo*
news *notizie*
newspaper *giornale*
nine *nove*
not *non*
to note *osservare*
nothing *niente, nulla*
nurese *infermiera*

OF *di*
office *ufficio*
on *su*
once *una volta*
one *un, una*
to open *aprire*
open *aperto*
or *o*
order *ordine*
other *altro*
our *nostro, -a, -i, -e* 14
to owe *dovere*

PACKET *pacchetto*
page *pagina*
parcel *pacco*
parents *genitori*
park *parco*
party *ricevimento*
to pass *passare*
to pay *pagare*
perhaps *forse*
person *persona*
photo *foto*
place *posto*
plant *pianta*
plate *piatto*
to play *giocare*
please *per piacere*
to please *piacere*
police *polizia*
portion *porzione*
to pray *pregare*
precise *preciso*
present *regalo*
prevention *prevenzione*
prize *premio*

product *prodotto*
programme *programma*
to promise *promettere*
puncture *scoppio*
pupil *allievo*

QUIET *tranquillo*

RARE *raro*
ready *pronto*
reason *ragione*
record *disco*
red *rosso*
regularly *regolarmente*
relation *parente*
to repeat *ripetere*
to reply *rispondere*
report *rapporto*
retreat *ritirata*
rice *riso*
river *fiume*
road *strada*
room *stanza*
rose *rosa*
rule *regola*
to run *correre*

TO SAIL *navigare*
sailor *marinaio*
Saturday *sabato*
to say *dire*
sea *mare*
seat *posto*
second *seconda*
to see *vedere, ricevere*
to send *mandare*
to serve *servire*
seven *sette*
several *parecchi*
she *lei, essa, ella* 4
shop *bottega, negozio*
short *corto*
sign *cartello*
to sing *cantare*
sister *sorella*
six *sei*
sky *cielo*
to sleep *dormire*
slow *lento*
to smoke *fumare*
soldier *soldato*

some *alcuni, qualche* 82
somebody *qualcuno*
someone *qualcosa*
something *qualchecosa*
son *figlio*
song *canto, canzone*
soon *presto*
sorrow *dolore*
I am sorry *mi dispiace*
space *spazio*
to speak *parlare* 18
stairs *scale*
star *stella*
station *stazione*
to stay *stare* 52
stick *stecco*
strange *strano, raro*
stranger *straniero*
strawberry *fragola*
student *studente*
subject *materia*
suitsace *valigia*
Sunday *domenica*
supper *cena*
supplies *rifornimenti*
surprise *sorpresa*
sweet *caramella*
swing *altalena*

TO TAKE *prendere*
to talk *parlare*
taxi *tassi*
to teach *insegnare*
teacher *maestro*
telephone *telefono*
television *televisione*
to tell *dire, racontare*
ten *dieci*
tent *tenda*
that (conj.) *che* 47
that (one), those
  *quello, -a, -i, -e* 52 *ciò*

thank you *grazie*
the *il, la* etc. 6, 7
their *loro* 14
them (dir. obj.) *li, le* 35
then *poi*
they *loro, essi, esse* 4
thick *spesso*
third *terzo*
this (one), these
  *questo, -a, -i, -e* 52
three *tre*
Thursday *giovedì*
time *tempo*
to *a*
today *oggi*
tomorrow *domani*
too much *troppo*
town *città*
train *treno*
training *allenamento*
treatment *cura*
Tuesday *martedì*
to turn off *spegnare*
to turn on *accendere*
twenty *venti*
two *due*
tyre *gomma*

UNCLE *zio*
to understand *capire*
us (dir. obj) *ci* 35

TO VERIFY *accertare*
very *molto*
village *villagio*
to visit *recarsi, visitare*

TO WAIT *aspettare*
to want *volere* 62

water *acqua*
to get washed *lavarsi*
we *noi*
to wear *portare, mettere*
weather *tempo*
Wednesday *mercoledì*
week *settimana*
well *bene*
what? *che (cosa)* 38
where *dove*
which? *quale* 38
white *bianco*
who *chi* 38
who, whose, whom, which *cui, che* 47
whoever *chiunque*
wife *moglie*
wind *vento*
wine *vino*
to wipe *fregare*
to wish *desiderare*
with *con*
woman *donna*
word *parola*
to work *lavorare*
work *lavoro*
to write *scrivere*
to be wrong *aver torto*

YEAR *anno*
yellow *giallo*
yes *si*
yesterday *ieri*
you *tu, voi* 3
you (dir. obj.) *ti, vi, La, Li, Le* 35
your *vostro, -a, -i, -e* 14
your (fam.) *tuo, -a, -ói, -e* 19